CARS OF THE 1970s

Publications International, Ltd.

Contributing writer: Gary Witzenburg

Images from: Michael D. Allen; The Appel/Kapustka Archive; Darrel Arment; Automotive Hall of Fame; Don Badie; Roger Barnes; Barrett-Jackson; Ken Beebe; Derek Bell; John Bentz; J.R. Betson, Jr.; Mark Bilek; BMW Group; Randall Bohl; Joe Bohovic; Jan Borgfelt; Terry Boyce; Scott Brandt; Robert H. Brown; Bugatti Automobiles S.A.S.; Tom Burnside Motorsport Archive; Robert Burrington; Chan Bush; Gary Cameron; Thom Cannell; Caterham Cars; Bob Cavallo; Fred Chamberlain; Tom Clifford; Jeff Cohn; John Conde; Continental Auto Sports; Daimler AG; Mirco DeCet; Greg Don; Leigh Dorrington; Neil Ehresman; Ferrari S.p.A.; Sam Fiorani; Joseph A. Fitzpatrick; Steen Fleron; Roland Flessner; Ford Motor Company; Fox Valley Motorcars; Mitch Frumkin; General Motors Company; Chuck Giametta; Thomas Glatch; W. Goodfellow; David Gooley; Gary Greene; Sam Griffith; Ken Gross; R. Harrington; Jerry Heasley; John Heilig; Joe Heine Nissan; Don Heiny; Brandon Hemphill; Alan Hewko; Honda Motor Co., Ltd.; Reed Hutchinson; Jaguar Land Rover Limited; Greg Jaren; Milt Jenks; David Jensen; Jeff Johnson; Bud Juneau; Bill Kantz; Harry Kapsalis; Don Keefe; Milton Kieft; Bill Kilborn; The Klemantaski Collection; Jimmy D. Knapp; Nick Komic; The Collection of Tim Kuser; Automobili Lamborghini S.p.A.; Lotus Cars Limited; Dan Lyons; Pete Lyons; Don L. Magargee; Vince Manocchi; Roger Mattingly; Mazda Motor Corporation; Doug Mitchel; Ron Moorhead; Mike Mueller; David Newhardt; Robert Nicholson; Neil Nissing; Northwest Auto Sales; Nina Padgett; Panoz; Pebble Beach Concours D'Elegance; Jay Peck; The PIL Collection; Rick Popely; Albert Porter; Matthew Reader; Rob Reaser; Larry and Alice Richter; RK Motors Charlotte; Road America; Al Rogers; Jeff Rose; Scott Rosenberg; Rich Russo; Saab AB; Paul Sable; Steve Sadler; Saleen Automotive, Inc.; Richard N. Sandborn Jr.; Rik and Miki Schug; Ron Sessions; Tom Shaw; Shutterstock.com; Simon Lewis Transport Books; Larry Simon; Mark Sincavage; Gary Smith; The Society of Automotive Historians; Sheryl Sommers; Robert Sorgatz; Mike Spenner; Richard Spiegelman; Steve Statham; Alex Steinberg; Stellantis; Tom Storm; David Suter; Ernest R. Sutton, Jr.; Dennis Tanney; David Temple; Bob Tenney; Phil Toy; Toyota Motor Corporation; Lorraine and Bob Tracey; Ross Tse; Rob Van Schaick; Gary Versteege; Volkswagen AG; Volvo Cars Group; W.C. Waymack; Joseph Wherry; Jim White; Wikimedia Commons; H. Woodnorth; Nicky Wright; Paul Zazarine

ISBN: 978-1-63938-417-4

Manufactured in China.

8 7 6 5 4 3 2 1

Let's get social!
@Publications_International
@PublicationsInternational
www.pilbooks.com

CONTENTS

AMC AMX

AMC insisted that its AMX was a genuine sports car, and—while clearly derived from the Javelin pony-car with shared mechanicals, seats, and instrument panel—it was a short-wheelbase two-seater. It was reasonably comfortable with ample luggage space and, most importantly, could be V-8-powered. After bowing midway through the '68 model year, it was largely unchanged for '69 except that a Hurst shifter replaced its inferior factory linkage.

Changes were more substantial for 1970. A 225-bhp 290-cid V-8 replaced the 290-bhp 360 as standard, the optional 390 V-8 got freer-flowing heads and other improvements for a 10-bhp boost to 325, and a scoop on the restyled hood was functional when a Ram Air option was ordered. AMC also moved the park/turn-signal lamps to the grille, which left holes in the bumper that it said cooled the front brakes.

More effective was a revised front suspension that further improved the AMX's already crisp handling.

With a $384 "Go" package—which included E70x14 tires, front disc brakes, super heavy-duty suspension, limited-slip differential, Ram Air, and improved engine cooling—the 390 AMX was quick in the quarter mile and highly competent in the corners. "For the doubters, we can testify once again that the AMX feels like a sports car, drives like a sports car, handles like a sports car and therefore in our book (and that of the Sports Car Club of America) it is a sports car," said *Road Test* magazine.

But this muscular AMX survived just one year. The two-seater was gone for '71, and AMX became just an appearance option for the redesigned four-seat Javelin.

AMC SPIRIT AMX

The Spirit AMX was the performance version of the AMC Spirit, the much better-looking compact car that replaced the oddball Gremlin for 1979 on the same basic platform. Sort of a "poor man's Trans Am" powered by a 304-cid (5.0-liter) V-8, it boasted color-matched fender flares, a front air dam, a rear spoiler, a louvred rear window and a full set of decals including somewhat Trans Am-like hood flames.

With just 130 rated horsepower driving through a 4-speed manual transmission, its performance was respectable and its handling surprisingly good thanks to "Rally Tuned" suspension with front and rear sway bars, three-way adjustable Gabriel "Strider" shock absorbers, heavy duty front disc brakes and fat (for their day) radial tires on handsome Turbocast II rims.

Enjoying some success in International Motor Sports Association (IMSA) racing at the time, AMC teamed with BF Goodrich and its factory Team Highball to prepare and ship two Spirit AMXs to Germany to compete in the 1979 Nürburgring 24 Hour endurance race for FIA Group 1 (improved stock) cars. And this first American team to take on that grueling annual event surprised everyone by finishing 25th and 43rd overall, first and second in their class, out of 120 starters in seven classes.

The drivers were Team Highball's Amos Johnson and Dennis Shaw, factory Mazda pilot Jim Downing (who would later co-develop the HANS safety device), Lyn St. James (who would become the first woman to win the Indianapolis 500 Rookie of the Year award), A-List actor James Brolin, and this author/racer, Gary Witzenburg.

1972 AMC GREMLIN X

American Motors knew it couldn't compete head-to-head in every vehicle segment with the Big Three, but by the late1960s, it saw a potentially profitable opportunity in the compact field. After learning that both General Motors and Ford were planning to bring out subcompact import-fighters for 1971, America's smallest automaker decided to develop a viable competitor. The challenge was that AMC was even more cash strapped than usual given development costs for the coming compact Hornet and its impending purchase of Kaiser Jeep, so the answer came not from Engineering but from Styling.

Well accustomed to operating on tight budgets, Styling chief Dick Teague sold the idea of building a shortened Hornet. The Hornet then in development had AMC's most up-to-date engineering, and simply chopping 18 inches off its rear yielded the subcom-

pact they needed for very little additional investment. The front remained mostly Hornet, while the rear looked guillotined yet uniquely appealing with good cargo room under a large hatch window. Inside, the front seat retained its roomy (for a subcompact) Hornet dimensions, but the back seat (thanks to its foot-shorter 96-in. wheelbase) was tight.

AMC's Gremlin debuted on April Fool's Day, 1970, beating Chevy's Vega and Ford's Pinto to market by half a year. Prices started at $1,879 for a no-back-seat base model. Our pictured car is a 1972 Gremlin with the X package (body stripes, slotted steel wheels, an upgraded interior, vinyl bucket seats and sport steering wheel) powered by a 135-bhp 232-cid (3.8-liter) six driving through an optional Chrysler-built Torque-Command three-speed automatic.

1970–74 AMC JAVELIN

Javelin was restyled front and rear for 1970, but it would be a one-year-only design. A new front suspension featured ball joints, upper and lower control arms, coil springs, and shock absorbers above the upper control arms as well as trailing struts on the lower control arms. Two new AMC V-8s were a base 304 cid and an optional 360 cid replacing the old 290 and 343 V-8s. The top optional 390 continued and was upgraded to 325 bhp and 425 pound feet of torque. Also new (with a "Go Package" option) was a "power blister" hood with two large openings for functional cold ram-air induction. This package also offered front disc brakes, a dual exhaust system, heavy-duty suspension with anti-sway bar, im-

proved cooling, 3.54:1 rear axle and wide Goodyear white-letter performance tires on styled wheels.

The 1971 longer, lower, wider and heavier second-generation Javelin was aggressively restyled with an integral roof spoiler and sculpted fender bulges (to accommodate large racing tires) on a one-inch longer wheelbase. Engine choices included a 232-cid inline six and a 401-cid V-8, the latter rated at 330 bhp and 430 pound feet. A BorgWarner T-10 four-speed manual transmission came with a Hurst floor shifter. Also, with the two-seat AMX gone, that label was affixed to a premium high-performance Javelin advertised as "the closest thing you can buy to a Trans-Am champion." The 3,244-pound 1971 Javelin AMX with a 401 V-8 could run mid-14-sec. 1/4-miles at 93 mph on low-lead gas.

Javelin offered styling tweaks for 1972, along with engine power ratings downgraded to more accurate Society of Automotive Engineers (SAE) net horsepower figures. Yet AMC achieved record sales that year by focusing on quality and an innovative "Buyer Protection Plan" warranty. Beginning that March, a bold Pierre Cardin interior design was offered for $84.95, and 4,152 Javelins were sold with it in 1972 and '73. And after Javelins won Trans-Am racing titles in 1971 and 1972, AMC offered a limited run of "Trans Am Victory" edition 1973 Javelins.

Javelins got five-mph bumpers for 1973 and further downgraded engine ratings due to tougher emissions standards. The 401-cid V-8 was rated at net 255 bhp (yet could do 0–60 mph in 7.7 seconds), and *Road Test* magazine tested a 401 cid, four-speed

manual 1973 Javelin SST at 15.5 seconds at 91 mph in the 1/4-mile. Javelin production for the 1973 model year totaled 30,902 units including 5,707 AMXs.

By post-fuel-crisis 1974, the automobile marketplace had changed. Chrysler dropped its pony cars, Ford replaced its Mustang with a smaller (Pinto-based) four-cylinder version, and other automakers downsized engines. Javelin production reached a second-generation high of 27,696 units, of which 4,980 were AMX models, but the car was canceled that fall.

1978 BMW M1

Unveiled in late 1978, the M1 was BMW's first mid-engine production car, though it was conceived at least five years earlier as a Porsche 911-beater in production-class racing. Lacking mid-engine experience, BMW contracted this beauty's chassis development to Lamborghini and its body design to Giorgetto Giugiaro's Ital Design. The resulting two-seat coupe wore a fiberglass skin over a complex multitube chassis powered by a special version of its trademark 3.5-liter inline six with dual overhead cams, four valves per cylinder, and a strong 277 DIN horsepower delivered through a five-speed manual transaxle. Its suspension was all-independent, and it rolled on uncommonly large (for the time) 16-inch wheels and tires.

A few 470-bhp racing versions were built for Europe's 1979–80 "Procar" support series, and a handful of 3.2-liter turbocharged M1s claimed a whopping 850 bhp. But BMW lost interest and discontinued the M1 in 1981 after total production of just 450 units. Today, it's a highly sought-after collector car capable of 0-60 mph in 5.5 seconds and 160-mph top speed.

1970–75 BMW 1600–2002

The 1600–2 (the "-2" for "2-door") was an entry-level BMW smaller and less expensive than the New Class Sedan on which it was based. It debuted at the Geneva Motor Show in 1966 and was sold through 1975 with the designation simplified to "1602" in 1971. Its 1.6-liter four produced 84 bhp and 96 pound feet of torque. American importer Max Hoffman asked BMW for a sporting version for the United States, and the resulting 2.0-liter model became the 2002.

In 1971, the 02 Series received a facelift, and a Touring version became available with all engine sizes at the time, including the 2002 tii as the replacement for the fuel-injected 2002 ti. The 2002 tii used a 128-bhp fuel-injected version of the engine capable of 115 mph, but just 422 examples were built. Other upgrades included wraparound bumpers, a 2-piece instrument cluster and new seats.

Exterior changes for 1973 included revised grille and taillamps (except for Touring models and in the

United States, which maintained round taillamps), but U.S. models received those revisions for 1974. A 2002 Turbo was introduced just before the 1973 oil crisis, so only 1,672 were built. The 2002 was replaced for 1975 by the much more civilized and stylish 3-Series.

BMW 3 SERIES

Successor to the 1600–2002, the 3 Series is a line of compact executive cars built by German automaker BMW since May 1975. The first generation was available only as a two-door sedan, but the model range expanded over time to include four-door sedan, two-door convertible, two-door coupé, five-door estate, five-door liftback, and three-door hatchback body styles. All models were initially powered by carbureted four-cylinder engines, but fuel-injected models were introduced in late 1975 and six-cylinder engines added in 1977. The 3 Series has been BMW's best-selling model and has won numerous awards throughout its history.

BMW 3.0 CSL

"This performance coupé from the 1970s was . . . the most handsome touring car of its era," wrote Djordje Sugaris for sportscardigest.com. Its 2800 CS predecessor launched in 1968, and 1971 brought the 3.0 CS and the lightweight, fuel-injected 3.0 CSi (Coupé Sport Liecht). Designed and developed with racing in mind, the CSi's 1971–75 production was outsourced to Karmann with a total of 1265 examples built, none originally intended for North America.

Sugaris noted, "The M30 engine of the 3.0 CSL had three iterations, each catering to a set of regulations and BMW Motorsport's racing goals." The first 180-bhp carbureted version went into the first 169 cars. Then came a slightly larger (3003 cc, to qualify for over-3.0-liter racing) Bosch D-Jetronic fuel-injected variant good for 197 bhp. The third version, with Bosch L-Jetronic injection and displacement increased to 3153 cc, offered 203 bhp beginning in 1973. All three drove through a Getrag four-speed manual gearbox and a limited-slip differential.

The 1973 CSL looked like a street-legal race car with its front bumper replaced by a deep air dam, two rubber fins stretching almost full length on either side of the hood and spoilers on the roof and rear deck. Since bolt-on spoilers were illegal in Germany at the time, they were packed inside the trunk for owners to install themselves.

"The race car was thoroughly reworked to be way more powerful, more aerodynamically efficient and considerably lighter," Sugaris wrote. With its 3.2-liter inline six bumped to 3.5 liters, ultimately with four valves per cylinder, the CSL won European Touring Car Championship (ETCC) driver's and manufacturer's titles its first year out in 1973 as well as a class win in the 1973 Le Mans 24-Hour. After that, it won every ETCC title from 1974 to 1979 and scored U.S. wins at Sebring, Daytona, and Talladega.

Wheeler-dealer businessman Malcolm Bricklin decided that America wanted a "safety" sports car, but his underdeveloped Bricklin SV-1 (Safety Vehicle 1) arrived in early 1974 and died late the following year. Powered by first an AMC 360 V-8, then a Ford 351, its gullwing-door body was a novel color-impregnated acrylic backed by fiberglass. While it did perform well in crash tests, it was heavy, thirsty, cramped, less than sports-car agile, poorly built and over-priced. Just under 3,000 were built.

BRICKLIN SV-1

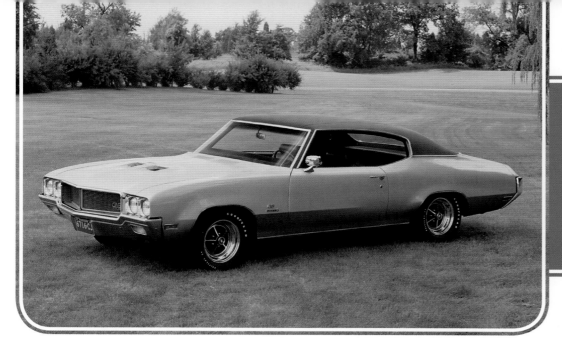

Buick's mid-size Skylark line again offered two GS performance models powered by a choice of 325-bhp 350-cid V-8 or big-valve, hot-cam 350-bhp 455 that replaced the previous 400-cid V-8. For the hottest version, buyers could opt for a $199 Stage 1 performance package for the 455, which added higher compression, a higher-lift cam and even-larger valves. It was rated at 360 bhp and the same muscular 510 pound-feet of torque as the regular 455. With either the four-speed manual or available automatic, a 3.64:1 Positraction rear axle delivered that prodigious torque to the pavement.

The 1970 GSX with the optional 455-cid Stage 1 V-8 was Buick's ultimate supercar. Among other things, this package added upgraded suspension, a hood-mounted tachometer, stripes and spoilers. Apollo White or Saturn Yellow were the only available colors. Of the 687 1970 GSXs built, 488 were ordered with the $113 Stage 1 upgrade. The fact that even GM's otherwise conservative, upscale Buick Div. offered a car as outlandish as the GSX is evidence of how thoroughly muscle-car enthusiasm had taken hold by 1970.

1970 BUICK GSX

1971 BUICK GSX AND GS 455

All 1971 Buick Skylarks got minor styling tweaks including a revised grille texture and new front and rear bumpers. There was just one GS (Gran Sport) series, and the high-performance Stage 1 package was ordered on only 801 GS coupes and 81 convertibles, a sign of waning popularity of muscle cars. A 260-bhp small-block 350-cid V-8 was standard, a 315-bhp 455 optional and a 345-bhp 455 available in Stage 1 trim, all detuned for low-lead fuel. The GSX was downgraded to an option package—bodyside stripes, hood paint, GSX emblems and rear spoiler—but color availability expanded from two to six and its front and rear spoilers, hood tachometer, and sport mirrors became optionally available on any GS model. A 1971 Stage 1 tested by *Motor Trend* did the quarter-mile in 14.7 seconds at 92.5 mph, ¾-sec. and eight mph slower than the 1970 GSX tested by *Road Test*. The GSX survived into 1972 but was dropped after a run of just 44 cars.

1971 BUICK RIVIERA

As General Motors' first "personal luxury" car, the 1963 Riviera was highly praised upon its high-profile debut. Its 1970 restyle incorporated design cues from (GM Design VP) Bill Mitchell's 1968 "Silver Arrow II" concept car, and its engine was upgraded to 455 cid, Buick's largest V-8 to date, rated at 370 bhp gross (245 bhp net) and over 500 pound feet of torque.

Then it was radically redesigned for 1971 with dramatic "boat-tail" styling inspired by the 1963 Corvette coupe. The only available engine was the 455 V-8 (with compression lowered to meet emissions standards), which delivered 255 SAE net bhp or 265 with a Gran Sport (GS) package. Performance remained reasonably brisk at 8.1 seconds 0–60 mph for the GS. Riviera sales dropped to 33,810 for 1971, lowest to date.

The 1972 Riv got a new egg-crate grille and more substantial front bumpers anticipating five-mph impact legislation, and sales remained stagnant at 33,728, suggesting that the boattail deck might be too radical. So, it was blunted and shortened for 1973 with taillamps moved to the bumper. The grille switched back to horizontal slats, the front park lamps were integrated into the headlamps and wrapped around the corners, and the front bumper was thicker with bumper guards to meet '74 standards. The now 250-bhp GS engine became standard with 260 available in a Stage One package. "Gran Sport" was a separate handling package with a rear stabilizer bar, JR78-15 steel-belted (whitewall) radial tires and a tuned "radial roadability" suspension. These changes led to just a marginal increase in sales to 34,080.

1972 BUICK GS

The high-performance GSX—touted since its 1970 debut as Buick's answer to Pontiac's GTO Judge, Oldsmobile's 4-4-2 W-30, and Chevrolet's Chevelle SS—was discontinued after Buick built just 8,575 GS (Gran Sport) models for 1972. The facts that Buick dropped its prices by $60-$70 and a large sliding fabric sunroof was offered as a novel option didn't help much, if at all, as muscle-car appeal was dying. The GS hardtop started at $3,225, the convertible at $3,406, and just 852 examples were built. The Stage 1 455 (down to a rated 270 bhp) remained available and quick at 5.8 seconds 0–60 and 14.1 at 97 mph for the quarter mile, as tested by *Motor Trend*.

1973 BUICK GS

When all General Motors intermediates were redesigned for 1973, Buick resurrected the Century name for its version. GS (Gran Sport) models were based on the new Colonnade coupe, and the basic GS package with special badging and five-spoke wheels added $173 to the Century coupe's $3,057 list price. The 455-cid V-8 was available in all Century coupes, but the 270-bhp Stage 1 version was a GS exclusive.

Priced at $546, it boasted a hotter cam and heads, Quadra-Jet carburetor, twin-snorkel air cleaner and dual exhausts. Only seven were built with manual transmission; all others with the THM 400 automatic. Though not as potent as earlier Stage 1 Gran Sports, Buick's new '73 edition was among the rarest, with just 728 built. Total 1973 GS production was 6,637, 4,930 with the 350-cid V-8 and 728 with the 455.

1974 BUICK RIVIERA

While carrying over the platform, mechanicals and some body panels from the 1971–73 Gen III Riviera, Buick replaced its controversial "boat-tail" roofline with a more conventional "Colonnade" treatment in line with its LeSabre and Electra brethren for '74. This look featured wide B pillars, fixed "opera" windows, an optional half-vinyl landau roof and a novelty that later became federally mandated: two high-mounted taillights below the rear window. Its 455 V-8 lost more power, dropping to 230 net bhp standard and 245 Stage One. But this revised styling did not improve sales, which (also hurt by the 1973 energy crisis) fell to 20,129 for 1974.

For 1975, the Riviera received a new front look with a vertical-bar grille. The standard engine's output dipped again to 205 bhp, and the Stage One performance package was dropped, but the Gran Sport handling package continued. Sales for 1975 were a dismal 17,306 and improved just slightly to 20,082 for 1976.

1977–1979 BUICK RIVIERA

Along with all GM "full-size" cars, Buick downsized the Riviera for 1977 onto a new, smaller B-body platform and became essentially a LeSabre coupe with different styling. Its wheelbase was down 6.1 in. to 115.9 in., its overall length down 4.8 in. to 218.2 in., and its weight down some 660 pounds vs. the '76. The 455 engine was replaced by either a 155-bhp 350-cid Buick or a 185-hp 403-cid Oldsmobile V-8, while California models got a 170 bhp Oldsmobile 350. And, unlike its front-wheel-drive Cadillac Eldorado and Oldsmobile Toronado cousins, it remained rear-wheel drive. The Riviera was a placeholder until the all-new E-body personal luxury coupes would be ready for 1979. Sales rose slightly to 26,138 for 1977, then fell to 20,535 for '78. This included 2,889 "LXXV" model 1978 Rivs that celebrated Buick's 75th anniversary.

The 1979 model year brought Buick's first front-wheel-drive Riviera and the brand's first-ever front-drive model. Built on a 114-in. wheelbase, it once again shared its platform and mechanicals with

Cadillac's Eldorado and Olds' Toronado. The Buick 350 and Olds 403 V-8s were dropped, but the Olds 350 remained along with a new 185-bhp 3.8-liter turbocharged Buick V-6 in the Riviera S-Type that would be shared with the Regal Sport Coupe turbo for 1980. The 1979 Riviera was *Motor Trend*'s Car of the Year, and sales more than doubled to 52,181.

1971 CADILLAC ELDORADO

Following its 1967 introduction, Cadillac's front-wheel-drive Eldorado got its first redesign for 1971. Though just a half-foot longer and 45 lb. heavier, it was designed to look bigger than the 1970 models it replaced. Power was provided by a 500-cid (8.2-liter) V-8 rated at 365 bhp—all '71 GM engines had lower compression to accommodate no-lead or regular gas for lower emissions—and the suspension was softened to improve ride at some sacrifice in handling.

While Cadillac dropped its De Ville convertible for '71, the Eldo coupe gained a convertible companion—at $7,751, America's only luxury convertible. Eldorados had two features that were much copied during the '70s: a spring-loaded (for pedestrian safety) hood ornament and prewar-look coach windows on the coupes. Despite a UAW strike that delayed the start of production, 1971 Eldorado sales were a record 27,368 units, of which 6,800 were convertibles.

1972 CADILLAC DE VILLE

All Cadillacs were restyled for 1971, then received only minor alterations for '72. This generation would be the last of GM's giants—a downsized but still big de Ville would debut for 1977—and the '72 Coupe de Ville stretched 225.8 inches long on a 130-inch wheelbase. A small but welcome change was the return of the "V" under the Cadillac crest. A tradition since '46, the "V" was removed from de Ville and Calais for '70, much to the disappointment Cadillac traditionalists. Also for '72, all domestic automakers—in preparation for catalytic converters that needed unleaded gas—switched from gross horsepower ratings to more realistic net ratings. While it was a "paper" change that had no real effect on performance, the 472-cid V-8's horsepower rating dropped from 345 to 220. *Motor Trend* tested a '71 Sedan de Ville's 0–60-mph acceleration at 10.1 sec., and the '72 would have had similar performance.

1974 CADILLAC ELDORADO

The 1973 oil embargo dramatically altered the future of cars, trucks, and the auto industry in general. Cadillac had reigned as the undisputed king of American luxury cars since at least the end of World War II, but higher fuel prices (and potential future shortages) meant that luxury cars would have to be smaller and more frugal. The European competition was already smaller and offered better handling and better fit and finish quality than 1970s Cadillacs.

General Motors was already planning to downsize all of its cars over the next several years but for 1974 still offered the big cars that a majority of Americans aspired to own. The ultra-lux Eldorado's styling had been revised for '73, so its biggest change for '74 was the large, impact-absorbing bumpers required by federal regulations. The interior was freshened with a new instrument panel and cushions on the doors that Cadillac called the "soft-pillow" effect.

1976 CADILLAC ELDORADO

Eldorado styling was freshened for '75 with skirtless rear fenders, and four-wheel disc brakes became standard for '76. More importantly, the '76 Eldorado convertible was touted as the last ragtop built in America, and Cadillac sent it off in a blaze of glory. About 14,000 soft-top '76 Eldos were built, but many more could have been sold, and the final 200 were white commemorative editions. TV cameras rolled as the "Last American Convertible" rolled off the line. Speculators quickly bid prices well above the $11,049 sticker, and prices went still higher at auctions. Then reason set in, and values crashed. And the convertible's celebrated demise turned out to be premature. Chrysler was first to reenter the U.S. convertible market in '82, and Cadillac would follow two years later.

1978 CADILLAC SEVILLE

Introduced in 1975, Cadillac's Seville was 27 inches shorter, eight inches narrower, and nearly 1,000 lbs. lighter than a Sedan de Ville. But smaller did not mean cheaper; Seville was Cadillac's most expensive car short of the Series 75 limousine. It was designed and built to compete with luxury imports, and Cadillac did not cut corners on engineering or standard equipment. Cadillac also invested great care into the Seville's assembly, fit and finish, and its 350-cid V-8 used electronic fuel injection to achieve a good balance between power and fuel economy. Most magazine tests agreed that the Seville didn't handle as well as its European competitors, though it did handle better than most American cars. No one criticized its smooth, quiet ride, and almost no one complained (or even knew) that under its handsome skin lurked a lowly compact Chevy Nova unibody platform. Built during the height of the CB craze, the car pictured has a factory-installed citizens band radio.

1970 CHEVROLET
CAMARO Z28

Because they had to build it on the compact Chevy II platform, which preset certain dimensions, not every designer was happy with the original 1967–69 Camaro. But the stunning 1970 Gen II car more than made up for that and put smiles on everyone's faces. Its low, wide, sleek shape with round (Jaguar-like) parking lamps flanked by pronounced headlight pods, (Gurney Eagle Indycar-style) pointed rectangular grille and sloped rear roof virtually screamed "sport." It captured headlines when it finally arrived in February 1970 following an extended UAW labor strike, and the only downside was no convertible model. A selection of inline sixes and both small- and big-block V8s were available in other Camaros, but the race-bred Z28 came with a 360-bhp 350 small-block V-8 that gave it mid-14-second quarter-mile capability. Stouter suspension, a decklid spoiler and 15x7-in. wheels were also standard on Z28s.

1970 CHEVROLET
CHEVELLE SS

In 1970, it was all about power. The accelerating horsepower race being run (some contend) since the early 1950s crossed the finish line that year. With rising insurance rates for hot cars squeezing consumers and government emissions regulations facing manufacturers, what was left of the muscle-car era after 1970 was a cool-down lap by comparison. Chevrolet capped this golden age of go with a Chevelle SS powered by the most powerful engine it had yet produced, the 454-cid LS6. With an 11.25:1 compression ratio, it generated 450 bhp at 5600 rpm and 500 pound-feet of torque at 3600 rpm—enough raw power and torque to break 13.5 seconds in the quarter-mile. By comparison, available 396 V-8s (with displacement actually up to 402 cid) spun out 350 and 375 bhp while an LS5 454 made "only" 360 bhp.

1970 CHEVROLET
CHEVELLE SS 454 LS6

When GM lifted its displacement limit on midsize cars, Chevy responded with a monster 454-cid V-8 that started at 360 bhp and topped out at a ground-pounding 450—the highest factory power rating of the original muscle-car era. This ultimate LS6 454 came with an 800-cfm Holley 4-bbl. on an aluminum intake manifold, 11.25:1 compression, solid lifters and four-bolt mains. "In 1970, if you had to pick a regular-production, steel-bodied car from the Bowtie camp to go heads-up against a Street Hemi, it would've been this one," wrote *Hemmings*' Mike McNessor in 2017. "Which is exactly why most of these cars were ordered—to go rounds at the track or on the street." Chevy built 8,773 1970 Chevelle SS 454s, of which 4,475 were LS6-powered (the remainder with the milder LS5), but there is no apparent accounting of how many of those were hardtops, convertibles or El Caminos. When *Hot Rod* tested an LS6 SS 454 that year, it stormed to a 13.4-second quarter mile at 108.7 mph.

1970 CHEVROLET
MONTE CARLO

One product niche that Chevrolet had not contested with Ford before this year was the "personal-luxury" coupe segment that Ford had created with the 1958 four-seat Thunderbird. That changed in 1970 with the introduction of the Monte Carlo. A slick bit of repackaging, the formally styled, V8-only, two-door hardtop rolled on the four-door Chevelle's 116-inch-wheelbase chassis. It soon became known for having the longest hood in Chevy history and for being one of the division's few then-recent cars whose name didn't start with C. At $3,123 base sticker, it undercut the cheapest '70 T-Bird by $1,800, and the 130,657 Monte Carlos built that first year swamped its established Ford rival's production total. Among that number were 3,823 with the SS option that featured a new 360-hp 454-cid V8 and a handling suspension.

1970 CHEVROLET
CORVETTE

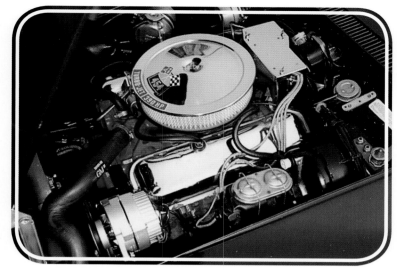

Corvette styling was little changed for 1970, the third year of its Mako Shark-inspired third generation. It got a bigger small-block V-8 for '69, reaching a new peak of 370 bhp from the available high-revving, high compression 350-cid LT-1 V-8, and a new ZR-1 option teamed the LT-1 engine with a package of special racing equipment—then a bigger big-block for '70 at 454 vs. the previous 427 cid. Two 454 versions were listed, but only the 390-bhp 4-bbl. LS5 saw genuine production. *Car and Driver* tested one 'Vette with the high-performance higher-compression aluminum cylinder heads, high-lift cams and

mechanical lifters) LS7 option good for a claimed 460-465 bhp. Though the magazine reported a sizzling 13.8-sec. quarter-mile at 108 mph, the LS7 was not readily available, and few (if any) other '70 Corvettes were so equipped. One reason was an auto workers' strike that delayed sales to February 1970 and nearly halved model-year production to 17,316 units, lowest since 1962. Base prices were $4,849 for the convertible vs. $5,192 for the T-top coupe, but convertibles accounted for just 6,648 units due to an accelerating sag in demand for droptop models throughout the market.

1970 CHEVROLET CAMARO

Delayed by a bitter UAW strike, the second-generation Camaro launched in February 1970—and therefore often called the "1970-1/2" Camaro—was produced through the '81 model year with mostly cosmetic changes for 1974 (to accommodate five-mph federal bumpers) and 1978. Beautifully restyled, it remained on the GM F-body platform similar to its Gen I predecessor with a unibody struc-

ture, front subframe, an A-arm front suspension and leaf springs on a solid rear axle. There was no convertible, just a sleek coupe with standard, RS (Rally Sport), performance SS (Super Sport) and road-racing-oriented Z/28 variants. Largely due to its late introduction, 1970 model-year sales at 124,901 were just over half of the 1969 total of 243,085.

1971 CHEVROLET
CHEVELLE SS AND SS 454

For 1971, all Chevelles got single headlamps (borrowed from the Monte Carlo) and a new rear bumper with round taillamps. The basic SS package offered a lot for $357—F41 handling suspension with front and rear stabilizer bars, power front disc brakes, wider F60 tires on larger 15-inch five-spoke wheels and a blackout grille, and SSs could be further spiffed with optional racing stripes and a cowl Induction hood. The changing muscle-car landscape saw small-blocks re-emerge in the form of two 350-cid V-8s—a 245-bhp 2-bbl. and a 270-bhp 4-bbl.—in SS models. But big-block power was still available.

To retain the hallowed SS 396 badging, Chevy had called its slightly enlarged 1970 402-cid V-8 a "396." But for '71, it was renamed "Turbo Jet 400" and was a $173 option, $50 less than the 1970 base SS engine. Top engine choice was the $279 hydraulic-lifter LS5 454 V-8 rated at 365 bhp. Interestingly, only LS5 cars carried external "454" badges, while all others wore simple "SS" insignia. Chevy built 19,293 '71 Chevelle SSs (including El Caminos), 9,502 with the 454 V-8.

1972 CHEVROLET NOVA

When Chevy debuted its front-engine, rear-drive compact Chevy II for 1962—just two years after its innovative but ultimately controversial rear-engine Corvair—many predicted that it would outlive Corvair. In fact, while the Corvair was gone after '69, the Nova (a Chevy II trim level that later became the model-line name) survived and prospered through 1979. Wearing the handsome third-generation body that debuted for 1968, the '72 was available as a coupe or a four-door sedan on a 111-in. wheelbase. They offered a choice of 250-cid I-6 or two sizes of small-block V-8: 307 and 350 cid, and an SS performance option featured the 350.

1972 CHEVROLET
CHEVELLE MALIBU

Chevy's mid-size Chevelle was designed to deliver family car qualities in a tidier, more economical package compared to its full-size stablemates, and a lot of people loved its style. It was supposed to have been completely redesigned for that year, but a UAW Astrike and other problems delayed the all-new models, and a revised grille horizontally split into thirds and single-block parking lights were about all that differentiated the look of the '72s from the '71s. The clear sales leader of this popular family of cars was the Malibu two-door hardtop, 212,388 of which were built for '72, all but 4,790 with V-8 engines. In distant second was the "sensible shoes" Malibu four-door sedan, which scored 48,575 sales. But the '72 Chevelle ended up ceding its top spot in the mid-size market to Ford's all-new Torino.

1972 CHEVROLET
CORVETTE STINGRAY

While Corvette's Mako Shark II-inspired design would last another decade, the '72 Stingray marked the end of an era. It was the last year for chrome bumpers front and rear, since federal bumper damageability standards would bring a new front bumper under a body-color skin in '73. It was also the last of the C3 generation with a removable coupe rear window, a pop-up cover over the windshield wipers, 1970-vintage flared wheel openings, rectangular parking lights and eggcrate grille and fender-vent textures. Detuned engine offerings were restricted to a standard 200 (net) -bhp 350 V8, a 255-bhp solid-lifter LT1 350 and a 270-bhp 454. And it was the final year for that LT1, which could be ordered with a $1,010 ZR1 performance option.

1973 CHEVROLET
CHEVELLE SS

The SS package was carried into '73 on the new Colonnade Chevelles. Though the SS option hung on for years in El Caminos, this was its final year on Chevelles. A black-finished grille, bodyside striping, prominent SS badging and a Monte Carlo-style instrument panel were all part of the package. Hefty front and rear bumpers were unsightly but necessary to meet new federal five-mph impact standards. SS buyers could choose from among three available engines: a 145-hp 2-bbl. 350, a 175-hp 4-bbl. 350 or a 245-hp 4-bbl. 454 big block.

1973 CHEVROLET
CAPRICE CLASSIC

Chevrolet's line-topping Caprice Classic luxury series saw its best year to that point in 1973 with sales totaling 275,258 cars. That strong showing was still just 43 percent of the number of more-affordable Impalas, but Caprice was gaining on its sibling and would overtake it by the end of the '70s. Sales leader of the line was the stylish $4,082 two-door hardtop with its distinctive concave rear window,

which accounted for 77,134 units. The rest of the six-model Caprice lineup included a convertible (newly promoted from the Impala series), a four-door hardtop, a four-door sedan (added in '72) and two- and three-row Estate wagons. Square taillights and government-spec front "crash" bumpers were the major appearance changes.

57

1974 CHEVROLET VEGA

Increasing import sales in the late 1960s convinced GM President Ed Cole that the division he once headed needed a cutting-edge subcompact to take on the world. Instead, he got the Vega. As maligned as the little Chevy was during its model-year 1971–77 lifetime, it's easy to forget that it was the product of some advanced but unperfected ideas in its engineering, manufacturing, and even its shipping. The 97-in. wheel-base car arrived as a stylish hatchback coupe, a notch-back coupe with conventional trunk, a two-door station wagon, and a sedan delivery version of the wagon, all powered by an aluminum-block 140-cid overhead-cam four that ultimately proved troublesome. Sporty GT and plusher LX models were added over time, and in 1974, Chevy put out a trio of patriotic "Spirit of America" models that included a Vega hatchback.

1974 CHEVROLET
CAMARO Z28

The 1974 Camaros wore new federally mandated five-mph bumpers front and rear, plus a redesigned grille and "sugar-scoop" head- and parking lamps, but the split-bumper RS nose was history. The base V-6 model stickered for an affordable $3,162, and an available LT trim level added a "more sumptuous interior and other elegant touches." The Z28 was powered by a 245-bhp solid-lifter 350, and bold hood and decklid stripes were a $77 option on about half of the 13,802 1974 Z28s built. Production for U.S. sales totaled 146,595, a huge improvement over 1973's 89,988. But the Z28 would go on hiatus after this year, returning as a separate model midway through the 1977 model year.

1974 CHEVROLET CORVETTE

When Washington mandated stronger "5-mph" front bumpers for 1973, unlike most cars that year, Corvette complied with a handsome soft, body color nose. But crash-enhanced back bumpers were not mandated until 1974, so the '73 retained its slim-chrome-bumpered rear look. Also significantly, Corvette rolled on standard radial tires for the first time. In another sign of changing times, engines were down to a pair of 350-cid small-block V-8s—the standard engine rated at 195 net bhp, and an optional 250-bhp LT1—and one 270-bhp Mark IV 427 big-block (all with much quieter hydraulic lifters). While power and performance were down, Corvette remained one of few real excitement machines left on the U.S. market. No wonder '74 model-year production was a best-yet 37,502, of which 4,629 were convertibles.

The Laguna Type S-3 got a Camaro-inspired, aero-slick slope-nose for 1975, and new slotted covers gave its "opera" windows a racier look. For NASCAR racers, the new nose provided substantial aerodynamic benefit for higher top speeds on big super-speedways. The 454-cid big-block V-8, downrated again to 215 bhp, survived through 1975 as a Chevelle option, but this would be its last go-around. It was not available in California or, curiously, in the Type S-3. In addition, the optional four-speed manual gearbox was no longer offered.

1974–75 CHEVROLET
LAGUNA TYPE S-3

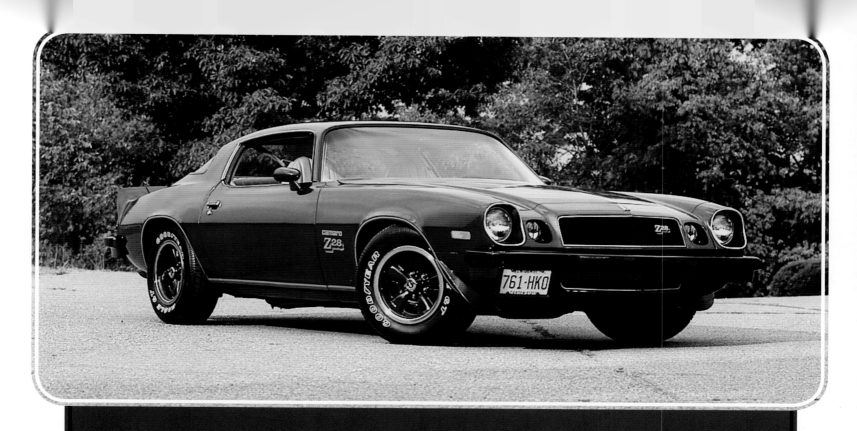

1977 CHEVROLET CAMARO Z28

Enthusiasts applauded the return of the Z28, which was revived midway through the 1977 model year as a stand-alone model instead of an option package. The $5,170 price included a raft of performance and image goodies including sport suspension, front and rear spoilers, and dual exhausts. Color-keyed wheels and bumpers, body striping and blacked-out grilles, and headlamp/parking lamp bezels further added to their performance look. Non-Z28s that year offered an optional 170-bhp version of the 350 V-8, but the Z28's same-size engine was bumped to a more respect-able 185-bhp and 280 pound-feet of torque via a higher-lift cam and other internal upgrades. Still, while its handling was as sharp as ever, the 185-bhp 350 didn't provide the spirited acceleration of past Z28s.

1977 CHEVROLET IMPALA

Even before the 1973 Oil Embargo and the resulting energy crisis, General Motors had decided that its full-size cars were too big, so development of trimmer cars was already in progress when the crisis made downsizing imperative. The 1977 full-size Impala and Caprice were 10 inches shorter and more than 600 pounds lighter than 1976 models, yet their interior roominess remained nearly the same. The new styling featured crisp lines that GM Design VP Bill Mitchell, called the "sheer look." As it turned out, this first GM downsizing program was a huge success with Chevy's big-car sales increasing 56.1 percent over the previous year.

1978 CHEVROLET CORVETTE

For 1978, America's sports car celebrated its 25th birthday with a new fastback roofline and rear window, numerous smaller changes, and a limited-edition Silver Anniversary option package. Horsepower continued to recover from its mid-decade nadir with the small-block amped up to 185 bhp standard and 220 optional. Still, year-to-year Corvette sales declined for the first time in a long while to just under 48,000 for the model run. One highlight of Corvette's 25th birthday year was serving as the 1978 Indianapolis 500 pace car, and Chevrolet built 6,502 Pace Car Replicas to celebrate that honor. Each wore special two-tone paint, glass T-top panels (a new option for other '78s), front and rear spoilers, wider tires, unique high-back seats and a set of "Official Pace Car" decals for owners to apply if they wanted the full race-day look. Despite their stiff $13,653 base sticker, Pace Car Replicas proved an easy sell, so much so that (to Chevy's dismay) some fast-buck artists knocked off counterfeit replicas.

1978 CHEVROLET AEROVETTE

Then-Corvette chief engineer Zora Arkus-Duntov very much wanted to produce a mid-engine Corvette. Beginning in the late 1960s, he developed a series of increasingly serious mid-engine Corvette concept cars—two of them Wankel rotary engine-powered—that culminated with this gorgeous Aerovette. Born as the V-8-powered 1970 XP (Experimental Prototype) 882, it later evolved into the twin-two-rotor Wankel-powered Four-Rotor

Corvette that debuted at the 1973 Paris Motor Salon. Then, after GM gave up on the thirsty and troublesome Wankel, its rotary engine was replaced by a V-8, and it was renamed Aerovette. In Duntov's mind, at least, it was close to production intent. But Chevy's conventional front-engine Corvette was doing just fine, thank you, and there was little leadership support to move to a more expensive and less practical mid-engine design.

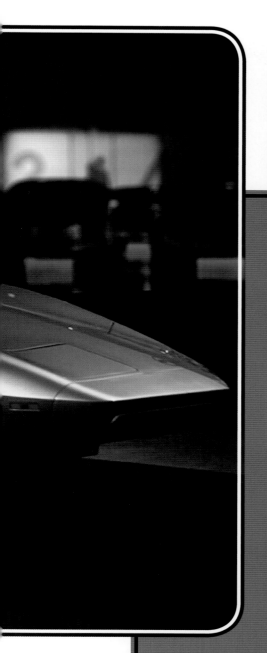

1970 CHRYSLER CORDOBA DE ORO

This Chrysler Cordoba de Oro concept car was unveiled at the Chicago Auto Show in 1970. Designed
by Elwood Engel, Chrysler's design chief from 1961
to 1974, it had a cantilevered roof with no A-pillars—
vertical supports in the window area connect roof to
body—and experimental, grille-shaped headlights.

Wedge design became popular with auto design-
ers in the late 1960s and by the 1980s eventually
made it to such high-end sportsters as the DeLorean
DMC-12, Lotus Esprit and Lamborghini Countach.
The Cordoba name would later be used on Chrysler's personal luxury coupe.

CHRYSLER IMPERIAL

Introduced in 1926, Imperial was Chrysler's top-of-the-line car for much of its history, competing with Cadillac, Lincoln, Packard, and even Duesenberg, Cord, and Pierce Arrow. It was spun off as a separate marque in 1955 (though always sold by Chrysler dealerships) to better challenge GM's Cadillac and Ford's Lincoln and remained separate until 1971, when it was again badged as "Chrysler Imperial." Then the "Chrysler" badging was removed again for 1974.

In 1967, Chrysler's Imperial Division moved from separate body-on-frame construction to shared Chrysler bodies, though with unique styling, a three-inch-longer wheelbase and (through 1973) very long hoods. But they carried over their unique front suspension with torsion bars longer than all other

Chrysler products and a rubber-isolated subframe crossmember containing the torsion bar anchors.

In 1974 and 1975, separate brochures were published, separate Imperial signs still stood above Chrysler dealerships, and Imperials continued with unique features such as hidden headlamps (since 1969), standard four-wheel disc brakes, and optional antilock brakes (since 1971). But their wheelbase was reduced to the same 124 inches as other big Chryslers.

Imperial took a hiatus in 1976, and the cars designed to be Imperials were rebranded as New Yorker Broughams (with exceptionally nice interiors) through 1978. Then the brand was resurrected for model years 1981–83 as a two-door luxury coupe based on the second-generation Chrysler Cordoba platform.

1975 CHRYSLER CORDOBA

Stylish "personal" luxury coupes were big business in the 1970s. GM had two hot entries with its Chevrolet Monte Carlo and Pontiac Grand Prix, Ford had Thunderbird, and Chrysler decided it needed a direct reply so began work on Plymouth and Dodge competitors. At the last minute, the "premium" Plymouth-to-be was given to Chrysler, resulting in the 1975 Cordoba. The styling mock-up differed only in detail from production models and laid the groundwork for what was truly the right car at the

right time. As the smallest Chrysler since World War II, the 115-in.-wheelbase Cordoba started at $5,072. All the required luxury touches were there, and the '75 Cordoba attracted more than 150,00 buyers, accounting for a full 60 percent of Chrysler sales that year. And Hollywood actor Ricardo Montalban took TV by storm in his role as the Cordoba pitchman. His exotic pronunciation of the car's name and available "Corinthian leather" interior helped capture public attention.

DATSUN 510

The Datsun 510 was a series of the Datsun Bluebird sold from 1968 to 1973, and outside the U.S. and Canada as the Datsun 1600. Its engineering—inspired by European sedans, particularly the 1966 BMW 1600-2—featured an overhead camshaft four-cylinder and four-wheel independent suspension with front MacPherson struts and rear semi-trailing arms. The 510 became famous for racing and rallying success outside Japan and paved the way for greater Nissan sales internationally.

The North American Datsun 510 had a carbureted 1.6-liter four rated at 96 bhp, front disc brakes and either four-speed manual or three-speed automatic transmission. Two-door sedan, four-door sedan and four-door station wagon variants were available. Best known in the U.S. for its motorsports success, it won Sports Car Club of America (SCCA) Trans Am Series under 2.5-liter class championships in 1971 and 1972 as well as numerous SCCA amateur wins.

1970 DATSUN 240Z

The Datsun 240Z was one of America's most talked-about cars on its 1970 debut, and no wonder. Priced from just $3,526, it offered the style and performance of sports cars costing thousands more, plus GT-like comfort and convenience. Riding a 90.7-inch wheelbase, the thoroughly modern Z boasted a 151-bhp overhead-cam 2.4-liter inline six with five-speed manual or optional three-speed automatic transmissions, all-around coil-spring/strut suspension, rack-and-pinion steering and front-disc brakes. Some critics said it had the burly charm of the late Austin-Healey 3000, while others applauded the smooth hatchback coupe styling and well-equipped cockpit.

Count Albrecht Goertz of BMW 507 fame contributed much to the design, which had elements recalling his earlier work for what became Toyota's 2000GT. Though not immune to rust, the unitized Z was far more solid than Datsun's MGB-like, body-on-frame roadsters of the '60s. If not Detroit-style muscular, the 240Z's straight six was very smooth and—helped by a modest 2,300-pound curb weight and sensible gearing—more than potent enough. With factory-backed teams under Bob Sharp and Peter Brock and a growing number of talented independent racers, the 240Z also piled up multiple victories in U.S. sports car road racing. Among many other notable wins, John Morton won SCCA C-Production national championships in 1970 and '71 driving a Brock Racing Enterprises Z like this.

Road & Track reported a respectable 8.7 seconds 0-60 mph, a standing quarter-mile of 17.1 seconds at 85 mph, and a 122-mph top end, plus 21 miles per gallon on-road economy. And it concluded that first Z test by predicting the Datsun would "establish a market of its own, [forcing] other makers to come up with entirely new models to gain a share in it." Americans snapped up 9,977 1970 Zs, nearly 27,000 in '71 and 46,600 in 1972, and global sales were equally strong.

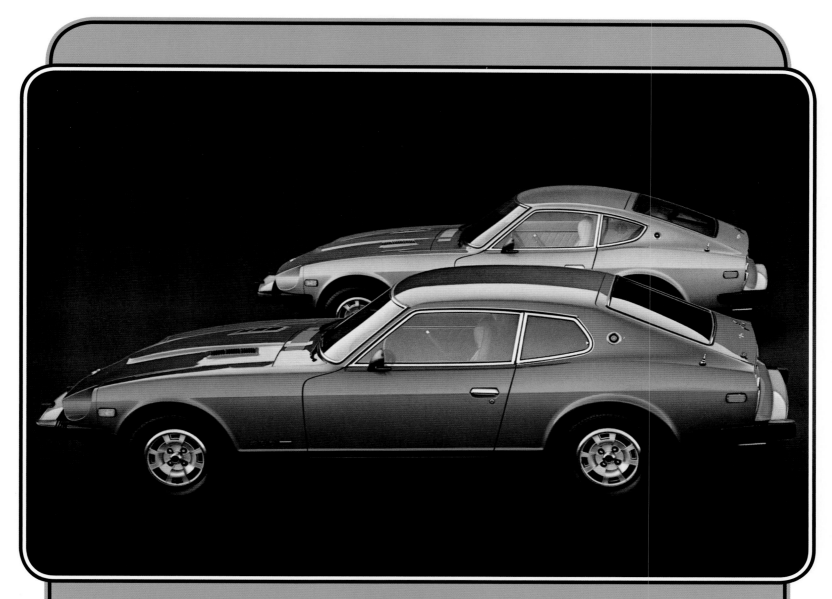

DATSUN 260Z, 280Z, 280ZX

Datsun's popular 240Z was updated in 1973 to become the 260Z. The new name reflected enlargement of the inline six from 2.4 to 2.6 liters to offset performance losses from tightening U.S. emissions standards. SAE net horsepower rose by 10 to 139, but its performance was somewhat diminished by weighty new 5-mph bumpers that also dulled handling a bit. The following year, parent Nissan added a 260Z 2+2 on a 102.6-inch wheelbase, which most thought looked less lovely than the two-seater, as this pairing may suggest.

With U.S. sales starting to soften, Nissan added more displacement and fuel injection for the America-only 280Zs that bowed in March 1975 with 168 bhp. That returned performance of the two-seater to near 1970 levels, though the car's handling still did not quite compare. The sportiest Datsun was clearly moving toward comfort-cruiser GT and would get there with the replacement 280ZX of 1978.

A "cutaway" view of the 260Z highlights the engineering and packaging of the original Datsun Z-Car. Note the simple but effective all-independent suspension with lower wishbones and coil-over struts. Note, too, that the power-train is placed so that most of its weight is behind the front-axle center-line—the so-called "front/ mid-engine" layout that tends to balance fore/aft weight distribution and optimize handling. Also visible here are the prominent U.S. 5-mph bumpers backed by long tubes designed to crumple in low-speed impacts.

Below: Though less impressive than early Zs on the street, the 260/280Z won SCCA national C-Production championships in 1974–76. This 280Z ran in 1978's new Showroom Stock-A class, which was won by neophyte driver Dale Fazekas.

1970 DODGE CHALLENGER

When Dodge finally got a legitimate pony car to race in the Sports Car Club of America's Trans American Sedan Championship, it built an even wilder version for the street. SCCA rules required makers to sell production editions of their track cars, and Dodge responded with the Challenger T/A. The race cars ran a destroked 305-cid version of Mopar's 340-cid V-8 with a 4-bbl. carb good for some 440 bhp, while street T/As stayed with the 340 but upped the ante with a trio of two-barrel Holleys atop an Edelbrock aluminum intake manifold. Despite the "Six Pak" carburetion and a host of internal reinforcements, the T/A's mill carried the same 290-bhp rating as regular four-barrel 340s, though true output

was closer to 350 bhp. Feeding it air was a suitcase-size scoop molded into the matte-black fiberglass hood. Low-restriction dual exhausts ran to the stock muffler location under the trunk, then reversed direction to exit in chrome-tipped "megaphone" outlets in front of the rear wheels.

The Challenger T/A was among the first production cars with different-size tires front and rear: E60x15s front, G60x15s rear. Modified camber elevated the tail to clear the rear rubber, giving the T/A a street-punk stance. Choices of manual or power steering and TorqueFlite automatic or Hurst-shifted four-speed manual driving through 3.55:1 or 3.90:1

gearing were available, and front disc brakes were standard. The Rallye suspension used heavy-duty everything and increased the camber of the rear springs. Thick side stripes, bold graphics and a black ducktail spoiler completed the look, though the cabin was standard Challenger R/T.

As it turned out, the T/A wasn't a consistent SCCA winner, and its street sibling didn't act much like a road racer, succumbing to heavy understeer in fast corners. But the intensified 340 and meaty rear tires helped production versions claw through the quarter in the mid-14s, a showing that would do any small-block pony car proud.

1970 DODGE
CHARGER R/T HEMI

Like a veteran heavyweight fighter using all his tools to finish strong in the late rounds, the Charger R/T returned for its last year with an unprecedented array of tricks. A new chrome loop front bumper was echoed by a fresh full-width taillamp housing, and R/T versions gained a simulated reverse body-side scoop. The color palette featured high-impact hues like Plum Crazy and Go-Mango, both borrowed from the new Challenger. New front seats were the car's first to qualify as true buckets, and a pistol-grip handle now topped the available four-speed's Hurst shifter. Carried over was the extra-cost SE (Special Edition) group with its leather upholstery, and Charger could be optioned for the first time with a power sliding sunroof.

Standard again on the R/T was the 375-bhp 440-cid four-barrel, but for those who didn't wish to shell out another $648 for the 425-bhp 426 Hemi, there was a new 390-bhp 440 with a trio of Holley two-barrels. Its cost and upkeep were friendlier than the Hemi's, torque was identical (at 800 less rpm), and few big cars were tougher in a street fight than a 440 Six Pack. The King Kong Hemi itself grew more accommodating with the addition of quieter hydraulic lifters.

No Charger offered a broader array of thrills and frills than the '70. But rising insurance rates and tougher competition caused R/T sales to fall 50 percent to 10,337 for the model year, and the new Six Pack outsold the Hemi by more than two to one.

1970 DODGE DART SWINGER 340

Dodge's compact Dart flaunted fresh front and rear styling for 1970. The previous performance top-dog GTS was discontinued, leaving the Swinger 340 to fill its role. The lone engine choice was Mopar's well-regarded 340-cid small block rated at 275 bhp. The Swinger 340 was offered only in hardtop form and came with a pair of nonfunctional hood scoops. Also standard was a tighter suspension, E7014 tires, chrome exhaust tips and a bumblebee stripe. Available extras included all-vinyl bucket seats, center console and styled steel "Rallye" wheels. The 1970 Swinger 340 drew 13,785 orders.

1970 DODGE CHARGER R/T

For 1970, Chargers had a new loop front bumper and a full-width taillamp housing. R/T versions gained simulated reverse-facing scoops at the leading edge of the doors. Inside, new high-back front seats were Charger's first true buckets, and a pistol-grip handle topped the available 4-speed Hurst shifter. R/Ts again had the 375-bhp 440 standard and the 390-bhp 440 Six Pack or the Hemi optional. R/T production fell by nearly half to 10,337, and the 440 Six Pack outsold the Hemi by more than two to one.

1970 DODGE CORONET SUPER BEE AND R/T

Dodge's mid-size Coronets (above) were facelifted for 1970 with a double-delta-loop front bumper, each loop housing a pair of headlamps and vertical grille bars. They remained on a 117-inch wheelbase, but the new styling added three inches to overall length. Performance models had a dual-inlet power bulge on the hood, and Ramcharger air induction with twin scoops was an extra option. At the rear, horizontally split taillamps echoed the look of the new front styling. Super Bees (right) still came with a standard 383-cid V-8, and the 440 Six Pack and Hemi were option choices. Coronet R/Ts looked

much like cheaper Super Bees from the front, but side scoops aft of the rear doors and a flat-black rear panel with triple-section taillamps provided visual distinction. The popularity of muscular Coronets was waning, and Super Bee production fell by nearly half to 14,254 while R/Ts registered a paltry 2,408 sales.

1971 DODGE CHALLENGER R/T

Challenger returned for 1971 with minor appearance (reworked grille and taillamps) and mechanical changes. The line was trimmed to a base hardtop and convertible, plus the R/T hardtop. The R/T also received body-color bumpers, simulated brake cooling scoops on the rear quarters and revised tape striping with large ID lettering on the nose and the bodysides near the C-pillars. With SAE net instead of gross power ratings, the 383 Magnum was down to 250 bhp net from its previous 335 gross. But unlike General Motors, Chrysler did not drop compression ratios in '71, so Challengers with the big 440 and Hemi engines were still very fast. But with the muscle-car market shrinking fast, Challenger sales fell dramatically with the 29,883-unit model-year total down by more than 60 percent vs. 1970.

1971 DODGE CHALLENGER INDY 500 PACE CAR

With the R/T convertible discontinued, all '71 Challenger ragtops were base models. But four Dodge dealers attempted to spur interest in Challenger by supplying cars for the 1971 Indianapolis 500 pace car program. As many as 50 Hemi Orange convertibles were prepared for use during pre-race festivities, two equipped with heavy-duty tires and other equipment—one as the actual pace car, the other as a backup. At the end of the parade lap, the untrained driver of the pace car—loaded with dignitaries—lost control as it was leaving the track and crashed into a press box, injuring several reporters. That was the last time the Indy 500 pace car driver would be anyone other than a retired racer or someone else highly qualified.

1971 DODGE CHARGER

Dramatically restyled for 1971 on a shorter 115-in. wheelbase, Charger was Dodge's only two-door intermediate offering. Six models were available: base 6-cylinder pillared coupe and hardtop and four V-8 hardtops—500, SE (with a customized roofline), Super Bee, and R/T. Ventless glass, concealed wipers, and torsion-bar front suspension were standard, some models featured hidden headlamps, and the Super Bee and R/T could have the "Ramcharger" hood with a vacuum-operated pop-up scoop. Base V-8 was a 230-bhp 318, Super Bees ran a standard 383 while the R/T had a 370-bhp 4-bbl 440. Both Super Bee and R/T models, along with the optional 426 Hemi, marked 1971 as their last model year. Charger prices started at $2,707, and the 500 hardtop coupe found 11,948 buyers with a $3,223 base price.

1971 DODGE CHARGER R/T HEMI

Losing two inches of wheelbase and gaining swoopy Coke-bottle contours, the 1971 Charger was a radical departure from its predecessor. And though its performance leader retained the R/T designation, the only '71 Charger with standard hidden headlamps was the luxury SE version. Standard blackout hood, faux bodyside air extractors, Rallye wheels, tape stripes, and optional front and rear spoilers made this to most eyes the most garish Charger ever, especially when wearing extra-cost colors like "Hemi Orange" and "Citron Yella."

With muscle in retreat, few expected to see the 426 Hemi V-8 on the 1971 Dodge order sheet, but there it was, with compression ratio and output down slightly to 10.25:1, 425 bhp, and 490 pound-feet of torque. The 370-bhp 440-cid four-barrel Magnum V-8 was standard, the 385-bhp 440 Six Pack optional, and the available Hemi cost $884, not including required extras such as the Sure-Grip diff. Four-speed manual was standard, TorqueFlite optional, and Hemi Chargers fed their dual quads with an Air Grabber hood scoop activated by a dashboard switch.

Though Mopar was holding out better than most against the anti-performance onslaught, Chrysler installed just 356 426 Hemis for '71—186 in Dodge Challengers and Plymouth 'Cudas, the remainder in redesigned Dodge Chargers and Super Bees, Plymouth Road Runners, and GTXs. Charger retained this body style through 1974, but Chrysler dropped the 426 Hemi after this year, making 1971 the requiem for this heavyweight.

1971 DODGE DEMON

Dodge received a compact Dart version of Plymouth's Duster for 1971, offered as a standard Dart Demon—the lowest-priced Dart at $2,343—or sporty Demon 340. A 198-cid Slant Six was standard, a 225-cid six or a 318-cid V-8 optional, and the Demon 340 followed Plymouth's successful 1970 Duster 340 into the junior-muscle market. Powered by a 275-bhp 340-cid V-8 mated to a 3- or 4-speed manual or a TorqueFlite automatic and sporting 14-inch Goodyear Polyglas GT tires (on optional Rallye wheels), Rallye suspension, larger drum brakes, and chrome exhaust tips, the Demon 340 was a devilish value starting at just $2,721. Dodge only used the Demon name for two years as it became the Dart Sport for 1973.

1973 DODGE CHARGER

No longer a muscle car, the 1973 Dodge Charger set a production record of nearly 120,000 units. Its minor changes included a new grille (no more hidden headlamps), 22-segment taillights and revised rear-quarter windows. With "personal luxury" coupes becoming hot sellers, the Charger SE—complete with stand-up hood ornament, six opera windows, and a landau vinyl roof—accounting for more than half of those.

1974 DODGE CHALLENGER RALLYE

Reluctant to invest any more money in it than necessary, Dodge did little to the Challenger for 1974. Rear bumpers were strengthened to withstand 5-mph shunts per government requirement, and the Rallye package was revised with a black-painted grille and "strobe" stripes trailing from fake fender vents. Substituting for the previous 340 as the performance option was a new 245 bhp 360-cid V-8. Sadly, Dodge pulled the plug on Challenger in mid-'74, after just 16,437 were built. Looking back, Challenger was not so much a weak "pony car" entry as it was a late one, appearing just as demand for such cars was starting to wane.

1974 DODGE DART

By 1974, Dodge's compact Dart had been growing in popularity for several years, so the division was understandably reluctant to mess much with such a good thing. Dart Sport models continued on the 108-in. wheelbase, while the hardtop and sedan stayed put at 111 inches. Proud of the Dart's wide appeal, Dodge offered eight models targeted at a wide range of buyers. The Dart Sport was the least expensive, starting at $2,878 with its standard Slant Six engine. An interesting Dart Sport option was the "Convertriple," which paired two separate extras: fold-down rear seats and sliding steel sunroof. Available as a two-door hardtop or a four-door sedan, a new line-topping Special Edition debuted mid-year. Dodge's answer to demand for luxury compact cars, it featured high-back seats, velour upholstery, plush carpeting and a designer SE hood ornament.

95

When Chrysler redesigned its compacts for 1976, Dodge's version was called Aspen. And in the era of "tape-stripe muscle," where looking cool on the street was more important than moving quickly down the strip, Dodge dusted off the R/T nameplate for its "performance" version. The Slant six was standard Aspen, but R/Ts were V-8 only with 318- and 360-cid versions available, the latter with 175 horsepower. This Aspen R/T also has the Super Pak option, which added front and rear spoilers, wheel flares, and louvered rear-quarter windows.

After a year as a Fury option, Road Runner migrated to the compact Volaré for '76. Then for '77, it was top of the heap of the two-door Volarés the marketing types called the "Fun Runners." Good for 150 horses, its standard 318 could be mated to three- or four-speed manuals or the TorqueFlite automatic. Still at 175 ponies, the 360 came only with automatic. The Super Pak option added front and rear spoilers, wheel flares, and quarter-window louvers.

1978 DODGE
ASPEN SUPER COUPE

For 1978, Dodge brought out the Aspen Super Coupe, which came only in dark brown with contrasting satin black hood, bumpers and lower body, plus huge wheel flares and a rear spoiler. Orange and blue stripes added to its racy look, which was backed up with 158-inch GT wheels, GR60 white-letter radials, rear anti-sway bar and a 360 4-bbl. V-8.

Aspen changed little for 1979, but the optional $651 R/T package added new strobe-pattern striping on the hood, taillight panel, and lower body, plus a three-piece rear spoiler, quarter-window louvers, dual sport mirrors, and cast aluminum wheels. R/Ts required an optional V-8, with the top choice still the 360.

1979 DODGE
ASPEN R/T

1979 DODGE MAGNUM GT

When demand for midsize two-doors moved from performance to "personal luxury" during the Seventies, Dodge's Charger adapted better than most by migrating to a posher platform shared with Chrysler's Cordoba for 1975. For 1978, the Cordoba-based Charger was joined by the new Magnum, whose claim to fame was a simple louvered grille and clear headlamp covers that retracted when the lamps were in use. Most Magnums were luxury XE models, but buyers wanting more performance could choose the Magnum GT with raised-white-letter radials on 15-in. wheels, retuned suspension and engine-turned IP trim. Unlike lesser Magnums, the GT could be ordered with a 195-bhp.360 4-bbl. Then rear-drive Mopar performance entered a long hibernation when Magnum was replaced by the Mirada for 1980.

1973 FERRARI 365 GT4 BB

Ferrari finally answered the Lamborghini Miura in 1974 with its own mid-engine supercar, the 365 GT4 BB. The initials stood for Berlinetta Boxer and signaled a new 4.4-liter horizontally opposed 12-cylinder "boxer" engine with twin overhead camshafts on each cylinder bank and a rousing 344 DIN horsepower. Such engines are called "boxer" because their pistons pump side-to-side like the arms of two people sparring. Bodywork, styled by Pininfarina, melded steel main panels with aluminum doors, engine lid and nose cover. Underneath was a complex chassis framework of rectangular and square tubing, plus the expected all-around coil-spring/double-wishbone suspension and four-wheel disc brakes.

Though rather heavy at 3,420 pounds, the BB decisively raised the bar for high performance, as expected of the successor to the fabled front-V12 Daytona. *Road & Track* ran its BB to 175 mph all out, "the fastest road car we've ever tested." Acceleration was equally vivid, with 0-60 mph in 7.2

seconds and the standing quarter mile in 15.5 sec. at 102.5 mph. Ferrari built around 400 BBs, then upped the ante in 1976 with the 512 BB. With an enlarged 5.0-liter engine good for some 360 bhp, R&T's test car clocked 0-60 in just 5.5 seconds and was estimated to reach no less than 188 mph.

1973 FERRARI 308 GT4

Though it replaced the Dino 246 in 1973, the 308 GT4 was quite a different "junior" Ferrari. For starters, it was a 2+2 on a 100.4-inch wheelbase (up eight inches from that of previous two-seaters) and the only body style was a coupe; no Targa-top available. What's more, styling was by Bertone, making this the first production Ferrari in nearly 20 years not shaped by Pininfarina. But the biggest departure was the new twin-cam V-8 replacing a V-6 in a similar mid-engine chassis. Sized at 3.0 liters, the V-8 was variously advertised with 205 or 240 horsepower in U.S. tune, 255 for Europe.

Regardless, performance was in the Ferrari tradition, with 0-60 mph available in a swift 6.4 seconds and a top speed over 150 mph. Perhaps because of its relatively sedate styling, this Dino isn't highly regarded among Ferraristi, though it sold well enough despite few improvements over a six-year lifespan. For many, the most important of those came in 1976, when Maranello inexplicably reversed itself and made a Dino an "official" Ferrari by adding prancing-horse badges to the nose, wheel hubs, and steering wheel. But the GT4's real significance is in introducing the engine that would serve a new generation of roadgoing Ferraris destined for far higher success.

1971–72 FERRARI 365 GTC/4

If the 330 GTC was regarded as the best all-around Ferrari in the 1960s, then its 152-mph 365 GTC/4 successor contended for that title in the 1970s. Like the 330 GTC, the "C4" was understated, refined, extremely comfortable and easy to drive with considerably more room inside. It was truly a Ferrari that could be used daily without compromise.

First seen at the 1971 Geneva Motor Show, the 365 GTC/4 seemed a replacement for the 365 GT 2+2.

Though technically a four-passenger car, its shorter wheelbase (98.4 in. vs. the 365 GT 2+2's 104.3 in.) and its low, sloping roofline made its tiny rear seats token at best. Ferrari compensated by having the rear seatbacks flip down to make a practical storage tray. Its Pininfarina coachwork featured a swooping fender line and flush-fitting glass. The V-12 had the 81m bore, 71mm stroke, double overhead cams, and 4390cc displacement of the Daytona's engine, but the hood was lower because its six Weber

carburetors were horizontally mounted rather than vertically atop the engine. Horsepower was listed at 320, vs. the Daytona's 352.

With power steering, power brakes a self-leveling independent rear suspension and excellent heating and ventilation, *Road & Track* believed it would be "a fine car for a cross country trip in any weather . . . Every new Ferrari model brings some noteworthy advance over previous ones," the magazine continued. "The GTC4's is mechanical refinement. Less mechanical thrash comes through from the engine room than in any previous Ferrari, and the controls are smoother and lighter than ever, making the car deliciously easy to drive well."

The 365 GTC/4 cost several thousand dollars more than the Daytona but equaled the faster two-seater in sales while both were offered concurrently. Still, though some 500 were made, its life span was less than two years.

1972–79 FERRARI
365 GT4 2+2, 400 AND 400i

The angular lines and airy greenhouse of the 365 GT4 2+2 marked a new design direction for Ferrari. Unveiled at the 1972 Paris Auto Show, this new four-seater looked very different from the lovely 1971-72 365 GTC/4—it was stretched over a longer (106.3-in. vs. 98.4-in.) wheelbase and had a wider track, allowing it to have usable rear seats—yet was otherwise nearly identical under this new skin. The GTC/4's 4.4-liter 320 bhp V-12 and five-speed transmission carried over untouched, and both had independent suspension front and rear with self-leveling units in back, power-assisted disc brakes, power steering and a robust tubular chassis. However, because of America's new smog and safety regulations, this car was never imported into the United States.

A revised version called the 400 GT appeared at the 1976 Paris show. Its V-12 displaced 4.8-liters, but its most important mechanical change was the gear-box. Ferrari adapted General Motors' state-of-the-art three-speed Turbo-Hydramatic for use with the V-12 to create the 400 Automatic—the first Ferrari available with a factory-installed automatic transmission—which proved a very popular move for owners. Externally, the five-speed-manual 400 GT and the 400 Automatic were nearly identical to the 365 save taillamps reduced in number from six to four and the addition of a small front spoiler. The interior, however, was substantially revised and much more luxurious with new seats and more leather trim.

These 400s would soldier on into the mid-1980s with their primary upgrade, introduction of fuel injection, coming in late 1979. The 400i (for injection) was offered with both the five-speed and the automatic, and fuel injection would spread to the rest of the Ferrari lineup within a year.

1973–79 FERRARI
365 GT4/BB, 512 & 512i
"BERLINETTA BOXER"

Enzo Ferrari wasn't blind to the success of the Dino, or to the market's yearning for a mid-engine 12-cylinder Ferrari. When he finally decided to make one, however, he surprised most everyone by using a "flat-12" engine rather than a V-12. The engine was dubbed a "boxer" because its pistons were opposed parallel to one another and moved like a boxer throwing jabs, a configuration Ferrari had used for years starting in its 1964 Formula 1 cars. The chassis was a semi-monocoque design around the cabin, with tubular subframes front and rear. Suspension was independent all-around.

"I very much liked the Boxer engine because of its space architecture," Sergio Pininfarina said. "For years, I had to fight with a high engine and a large radiator because the engine's height automatically

(dictated) the radiator's height. The boxer engine was lower, making everything easier." Pininfarina used 1968's P6 racing prototype as the design's starting point. Making the 365 GT4/BB's lower portions a different color from the top was a styling touch from the designer's 1956's Superfast I show car. "The idea was to 'cut' the car in two to make it look slender," he explained.

This was the world's first roadgoing flat-12 engine, but the fact that it displaced the same 4.4-liters as the Daytona's V-12 allowed Ferrari to use components already in production, including pistons and connecting rods. It was also the first in any high-performance sports car with camshafts driven by belts rather than chains, which made it quieter, less costly to build and easier to service. The transmission was offset to the left, with the gearbox located ahead of the final drive to provide room for the engine oil sump.

The prototype Boxer made its debut at the Turin Auto Show in 1971 with its top speed listed at a heady 188 mph, but it would be two years before it entered production. And the world that greeted Ferrari's fastest car was far different from the one that worshipped the Daytona. The oil crisis, political strife, crippling strikes and material shortages affected the Boxer's production process and build quality. And that may very well have affected its performance.

While every magazine met or exceeded the Daytona's 174-mph claimed top speed, none got close to the Boxer's quoted maximum. In its June, 1975 test, *Road & Track* called the Boxer "the fastest road car we've ever tested," but its recorded 175 mph was well short of 188. Acceleration was also disappointing at 7.2 seconds 0-60, some 2 seconds off factory figures. At speeds above 130, the front became light on undulating roads, and a slipping clutch and a troublesome transmission didn't help. Other magazines encountered similar problems, but when a 365 BB was right, it was really right. Mel Nichols clocked 0-60 in 5.4 seconds and 0-100 in 11.3 in a CAR road test that lauded the Ferrari effusively.

Refinement issues were addressed in 1976 with introduction of the 512 BB, the new name signifying the engine's 5.0-liters and 12 cylinders. Rear track increased 1.7 inches, and the body was 2 inches wider and 1.5 inches longer. The front end had a small chin spoiler, and NACA ducts helped rear brake cooling.

When *Road & Track* tested a federalized 512 in March 1978, 0-60 took 5.5 seconds and 100 took 13.2. Though the editors didn't record its actual maximum speed, they marveled at its ability to keep accelerating easily beyond 150 mph. "The 512 (is) the best all-around sports & GT car we have ever tested," they concluded.

1975–79 FERRARI 308 GTB

If the Ferrari world was turned upside down by Bertone's angular 308 GT4 in 1973, things were righted when Pininfarina's beautiful two-seat 308 GTB made its debut two years later.

"Based on the 308 Dino GT4 (but) with only two seats (the GTB) is regarded by many as the more natural successor to the much-loved Dino 246," England's *Motor* summed up for many. "The styling is the best to come out of Pininfarina for a long time." The Dino design comparison was apt. "Like the 206/246 Dino," acknowledged Sergio Pininfarina, "the inspiration for the 308's lines came from

the Dino Berlinetta Speciale we exhibited at Paris in 1965."

The 308 GTB was significant as the first non-12-cylinder road-going Ferrari to use the coveted Ferrari name. And the first Ferrari with a fiberglass body. Its underpinnings were identical to the 308 GT4's, but its wheelbase was shortened about eight inches to 92.1 in. Horsepower was quoted at 255 (though U.S. emissions regulations limited the first American-market cars to 240 bhp), and the European version used a dry-sump oiling system.

Road-testers fell in love. *Autosport*'s John Bolster marveled at its temperament: "The 308 GTB is a civilized car that anybody can drive." "Dino 246 fans, cheer up!" was how Paul Frere began a March 1976 *Road & Track* review. "There is a worthy two-place successor to your favorite car. And it's even better, faster, quieter and more comfortable."

Ferrari in early 1977 phased out the fiberglass coachwork in favor of traditional steel panels and in September introduced the Targa-topped 308 GTS ("S" for Spyder), with a removable center roof section covered in black vinyl and louvered panels instead of rear quarter windows. But U.S. 308s were rated at just 205 bhp because of ever-tighter American emissions rules.

1975 FIAT X1/9

Fiat took the 1290cc four cylinder from its front-drive 128 sedan and wedged it amidships in a tiny, wedgy, Bertone-styled, two-seat, Targa-top coupe to create the X1/9. Sent to the U.S. for model year '75, it wasn't as quick as it looked—about on par with a concurrent MGB—but was very nimble and fun to drive. Affordable, too, at around $4,600 to start. Early "federalized" models like this wore tacked-on rubber bumper pads.

1972 FIAT 124

The Fiat 124 Sport spider would survive the '70s with little styling damage, though emissions-prompted detuning reduced U.S.-model performance as time passed. Here, a Euro-market model circa 1972.

1970 FORD MUSTANG BOSS 302

If Ford was embarrassed that its finest Mustangs were the handiwork of the same two guys who developed the best Camaros, it never said so. GM executive Semon "Bunkie" Knudsen, who used performance to revive Pontiac, defected to become president of Ford in 1968 and brought along stylist Larry Shinoda, whose GM work had included the Z28 that had unseated Mustang as '68 and '69 Trans Am champ. Revenge would be sweet.

The Mach 1 was among their first efforts, but the most special '69 and '70 Mustangs drew on Shinoda's nickname for Knudsen: "Boss." Like the Z28, the Boss 302 was built as a Trans Am road-racing qualifier. Its heart was Ford's 302-cid V-8 wearing the high-performance, big-port cylinder heads being readied for the famous Cleveland 351 V-8. Fed by Ford's biggest carburetor, a 780-cfm Holley 4-bbl., the Boss's solid-lifter small-block was underrated at

the same 290 bhp as the Z28's 302. A Hurst-shifted four speed and 3.50:1 rear axle were standard, 3.91:1 and Detroit Locker 4.30:1 cogs optional. Underneath were racing-inspired suspension modifications, F60x15 Polyglas performance tires and power front disc brakes.

Shinoda's expertise in aerodynamics influenced the Boss's exterior. Mustang's phony fender vents were enclosed, a front spoiler was fitted, and a rear air foil and backlight blinds were optional. Blackout trim and stripes finished the look. Ford built 1,628 Boss 302s for '69, then 7,013 for '70 when quad headlamps were traded for double units flanked by fake air intakes, a "shaker" hood scoop was made available, and the engine got smaller intake valves and a 6000-rpm rev limiter. In Trans Am racing, Boss 302s retook the '70 crown from Chevy. Street versions weren't always as fast as a 302 Z28 but had more cornering power and a less peaky, more flexible engine. "The Boss 302 is a hell of an enthusiast's car," said *Car and Driver*. "It's what the Shelby GT 350s and 500s should have been but weren't."

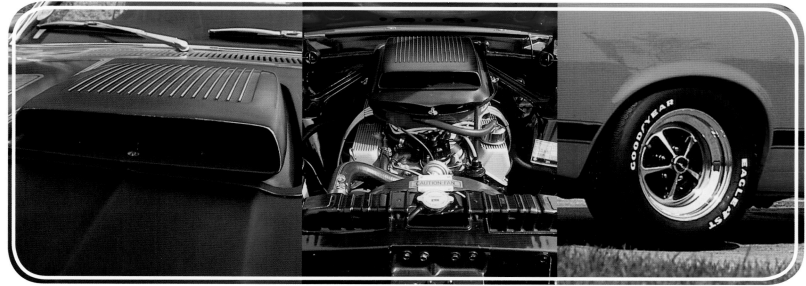

1971 FORD MUSTANG MACH 1

Redesigned for 1971, this was the biggest Mustang yet: eight inches longer, six inches wider and some 600 pounds heavier than the 1969–70 models on a new 109-inch wheelbase. Mustang's muscle mainstay remained the Mach 1, which was offered with a choice of six V-8s—the meanest being a 375-bhp 429 Super Cobra Jet. Mach 1s wore specific ID and trim, including simple flat-face hubcaps and bright trim rings. A NACA-scooped hood, body-colored front bumper, and honeycomb grille dressed up the front end.

1971 FORD MUSTANG BOSS 351

Though less fiery than the Boss models it replaced, the Boss 351 fastback was the quickest, most roadable '71 in the Mustang stable. A special High-Output 351 V-8 with premium internals delivered a solid 330 bhp through a four-speed manual transmission with Hurst shifter, good for 0–60-mph times under six seconds. Alas, hot-car demand was waning fast, and Ford fired the Boss at mid-season after building only 1,800.

1972 FORD GRAN TORINO SPORT

The redesigned Torino put on inches and pounds as it switched from unitized to body-on-frame construction. Base engine was a 140-bhp 302, and four stronger V-8s were available, but only the 351 4-bbl. could be mated with a four-speed manual transmission and a Hurst shifter. A 161-bhp 351-cid 2-bbl. turned an ET of 17.9 sec. at 80 mph for *Motor Trend*. The muscle-car era was receding quickly, but the Gran Torino Sport kept up the appearance of performance, a nonfunctional hood scoop and bodyside striping adding to its muscular look. Sports were all V-8-powered two-doors, but buyers could choose from the more traditional notchback hardtop shared with other Torino series or a racy Sports-Roof model that was a Sport exclusive, both starting at $3,094. The SportsRoof outsold the notchback by nearly 2-to-1.

1973 FORD GRAN TORINO SPORT SPORTSROOF HARDTOP COUPE

Prior to 1972, Ford's Torino ran second in mid-size car sales to Chevrolet's Chevelle, and the redesigned '72 Torino was larger and more like full-sized Fords than the previous generation. Traditional body on frame construction replaced the previous unibody, which worked with redesigned suspension to deliver a smoother ride, and all Torinos had standard front disc brakes—a rarity in the early '70s.

Torino buyers could choose a hardtop coupe, a four-door sedan or a station wagon in base or uplevel Gran Torino trims, the latter with a more distinctive grille and a nicer interior. The performance-look Gran Torino Sport was offered as a notchback hardtop coupe or a "SportsRoof" fastback unique

to the Sport series. All Gran Torino Sports were V-8 powered.

The bigger, better-looking, better-riding '72 Torino was such a hit that its production increased 52 percent over 1971, putting it well ahead of archrival Chevelle. Then the biggest change for '73 was a new front end designed to meet the federal requirement to withstand five-mph hits without damage. A flat front end with a girderlike bumper replaced the previous sculpted sheet-metal. Engines lost power as emissions standards tightened, and engine choices for the Gran Torino Sport ranged from a 137-bhp 302-cid V-8 to a newly added 219-bhp 460 V-8.

1973 FORD GRAN TORINO SPORT

When the government's "five-mph" front-bumper standard took effect for 1973, Ford's mid-size Torino received a bulky new front end to meet the requirement. Gran Torino Sport models continued, but the rakish SportsRoof made its final appearance in '73. Optional laser stripes and Magnum 500 wheels added pizzazz, but the hottest engine in the lineup was a 4-bbl. 429-cid V-8 good for just 201 rated horsepower.

1973 FORD MUSTANG

Mustang got a new grille and front bumper for 1973. To meet new limits on oxides of nitrogen (NOx), all '73 engines received a revamped emissions system with positive crankcase ventilation and exhaust-gas recirculation. This base Mustang hardtop wears the $51 Mach 1-like exterior Decor Group, which included striping, lower bodyside accent paint, a unique grille, and hubcaps with trim rings.

1973 FORD MUSTANG MACH 1

New bodyside striping and a bolder honeycomb texture on the rear panel, hood scoops and grille were the '73 Mach 1's main visual differences. This was the last year for Mustang's optional 351, now hanging on as a Cobra Jet with four-bolt main bearings, nodular iron crank, solid lifters and dual exhausts. Net horsepower was still-impressive at 275 but a far cry from a few years earlier. With 35,440 sold, Mach 1 was the second-best-selling '73 'Stang.

1976 FORD TORINO

The "striped tomato," a red '74 Ford Gran Torino Sport with a dramatic white stripe prominently featured in the '70s TV show "Starsky and Hutch" guaranteed the Gran Torino a permanent place in American pop culture. In March 1976, Ford's Chicago assembly plant began rolling out 1,000 copies of the TV car that depicted its red hue and white stripe fairly accurately. Missing from the replicas, however, were the TV car's aftermarket slotted wheels, which Ford did not offer or even try to duplicate. So, most owners added them. This Gran Torino, decked out like the TV car, is #474 of 1,000 and probably the lowest-mile example in existence.

1977 FORD
MUSTANG II COBRA II

Cobra IIs added color choices for 1977, including this black-and-gold combo that recalled the 1966 Shelby GT-350H Hertz "Rent-a-Racer." As in 1976, the base four-cylinder and a four-speed manual transmission were standard and the V-6 optional, but the available V-8 was the most popular choice. However, customers could not buy the four-speed manual with the 302 2-bbl. in California due to its tougher emissions standards.

1978 FORD
MUSTANG II COBRA II

Cobra IIs were little changed mechanically for 1978, but they got flashier stripes with large "Cobra" lettering. The aggressive spoilers, louvers and stripes "talked the talk," but with the top Mustang II engine choice still a 2-bbl. 302-cid V-8 packing a meager 139 bhp, Cobra IIs didn't "walk the walk." Cobra II Production slumped to 8,009, probably due in part to introduction of the even flashier (but no faster) King Cobra.

1978 FORD MUSTANG II KING COBRA

Surprising popularity of the Cobra II package prompted Ford to offer an even more outlandish stripes-and-spoilers appearance option for 1978. Though arguably well over the top, the King Cobra wasn't entirely for show, as the 302 V-8, power steering, power front disc brakes and handling-oriented suspension were included in the $1,253 package price. Not all that venomous, it could manage 0-60 mph in about nine seconds and the 1/4 mile in the mid-17-second range.

1979 FORD MUSTANG COBRA

An all-new Mustang thankfully replaced the Pinto-based Mustang II for 1979, and Ford pushed a performance theme with emphasis on handling rather than power. The available 140-bhp 302 V-8 and four-speed manual transmission were good for high-16-second quarter-mile ETs. Prices started at $4,071, and the Cobra package added $1,173 to the price of a base three-door hatchback. Included were the TRX suspension and Cobra ID, but the hood decal shown on this example cost extra. Mustang's 369,936 sales for '79 nearly doubled those of '78.

1973 HONDA CIVIC

The tiny but fun-to-drive 1973 Honda Civic brought the front-wheel-drive economy car into the American mainstream. And with the 1973 oil embargo hitting not long after its introduction, its timing could not have been better. Honda claimed up to 30 mpg and couldn't build these cars fast enough. Then, for 1975, Honda introduced the CVCC (Compound Vortex Controlled Combustion) engine that met tightening emissions standards without a catalytic converter.

1976 HONDA ACCORD

Following initial success of its subcompact Civic, Honda developed a larger stablemate and named it "Accord" to communicate the company's "desire for accord and harmony between people, society, and the automobile" (certainly one of the best car names of all time). It debuted (in Japan) in May 1976 as a three-door hatchback coupe on an extended Civic platform and sharing some Civic components and was powered by a 68-bhp 1.6-liter four with Honda's innovative CVCC technology to satisfy then-current emissions requirements.

One of the first Japanese entries with such standard features as cloth seats, a tachometer, intermittent wipers, and an AM/FM radio, the Accord sold well due to that level of content, its reasonable size and excellent fuel economy. A four-door sedan was added in October 1977 (a year later in the U.S. market), and Accord power increased when the 1.6-liter was replaced by a 72-bhp 1.75-liter four. An LX version of the hatchback that came with standard air conditioning, a digital clock and power steering was added in 1978.

1970–79 JAGUAR XJ6

The Jaguar XJ is a series of luxury cars produced by Jaguar, and from 1970 was the British marque's flagship four door model. Introduced in September 1968, the XJ6 was powered by a choice of 2.8-litre or 4.2-litre versions. In 1970, the old Borg-Warner Model 8 automatic transmission was replaced on the 4.2-litre XJ6 with a new Borg-Warner Model 12 that enabled performance-oriented drivers to hold lower ratios at higher revs for better acceleration.

In 1972, a long-wheelbase version provided four more inches of rear-seat legroom, and a high-performance XJ12 model packed Jaguar's potent 5.3-liter V-12. Capable of 140 mph, it was the world's only mass-produced 12-cylinder four-door and the world's fastest full four-seater. In all, 3,228 Series 1 XJ12s were built.

The "Series II" XJ received a facelift for 1974, and short-wheelbase models were discontinued. A 3.4-liter six was added for '75 while the 4.2-liter six and the 5.3 L V12 XJ12 carried over. Series II cars have a raised front bumper to meet U.S. regulations, with a smaller grille above and an additional inlet below the bumper. The interior received a substantial update,

including simplified heating and A/C systems replacing the complex, poor-performing Series I systems. U.S. XJ12s got GM Turbo-Hydramatic 400 transmissions, and electronic fuel injection replaced the previous carburetors. The 4.2-liter six followed with EFI for 1978.

When worldwide Series II XJ production ended in 1979, a total of 91,227 had been built, of which 14,226 were V-12 powered.

Based on Jaguar's XJ sedan, the new 1976 XJS was a 2+2 luxury coupe with a 102-inch wheelbase and a fuel-injected V12 with 244 horses. Though smooth, quiet, and quick, it was no sports car. Yet Group 44's race-prepped XJS won the 1978 SCCA Trans-Am series.

1976 JAGUAR XJS

1971 JAGUAR SERIES III E-TYPE

The much-modified Series III of 1971 boasted V-12 power, an artifact of Jaguar's super-secret "XJ13" racing-car project of the early 1960s. Replacing the venerable XK six cylinder, the 5.3-liter V-12 delivered 250 SAE net horsepower through a four-speed manual or a three-speed automatic transmission. Jaguar's longer, larger V-12 wouldn't fit in the E-Type two-seat coupe, so the only closed car offered was the higher-profile 2+2 first seen for 1966, and the convertible was reengineered on the 2+2 coupe's extended chassis, though it remained a two-seater. All Series IIIs got a cross-

hatch grille insert, reshaped tail, interior updates, wider wheels, and reinforcements to the unitized central structure and tubular front subframe.

Though heavier than previous E-Types, the V12 would do 0-60 mph in around seven seconds and well over 130 mph—real Ferrari/Lamborghini stuff. Yet it was far more affordable than those Italian supercars at around $7,000 to start in the U.S. Service access wasn't too bad with the E-Type's traditional lift-up hood/front fenders assembly, and this longer, faster E-Type lasted into 1975, when production stopped at 15,287, about a fifth of all E-Types ever built.

U.S Series IIIs delivered 14.5 mpg when the world energy crisis and gas shortages hit in late 1973, but that's not why it expired in early '75. The design was looking dated by then, and one U.S. magazine termed the Series III "a magnificent engine in an out-classed body." Then, too, Jaguar had become part of the increasingly troubled British Leyland combine and was working hard on a replacement sports-tourer designed for U.S. crash standards.

A team of Group 44 race-prepped V-12 roadsters captured the 1975 national SCCA B-Production championship, recalling Jaguar's rise to the pinnacle of world racing in the Fifties.

1971 LAMBORGHINI MIURA

Lamborghini's Miura improved in stages since its 1966 debut, and its last and fastest iteration was the 1971 P400SV. Compared to the previous Miura S, it packed 15 more horsepower at 385 thanks to bigger valves and cam timing and carburetor upgrades. Other alterations included a larger fuel tank, better engine oiling, vented (versus solid) brake rotors, and revised rear suspension geometry that raised ride height slightly but improved handling in concert with upsized wheels and tires. The cockpit also benefitted from upgraded instruments. The sensuous Marcello Gandini styling still looked great after six years so wasn't changed much except for visibly wider rear flanks (to accommodate the wider tires), a discreet ID badge on the tail, and layback headlamps without the "eyelash" trim on earlier Miuras.

With a top speed of up to 175 mph and acceleration to match, the SV was faster than a Ferrari Daytona and most every other street-legal machine. But Lamborghini was readying an even more outrageous supercar, so the Miura said goodbye in January 1973 when the last SV was sold. Ironically, an unprecedented world energy crisis that hit just nine months later seemed to spell the end for high-power "exoticar." But it thankfully didn't.

The 1971-72 SV's more muscular rear flanks and the rear-window slats became something of a '70s styling cliché for various production cars and as a popular aftermarket bolt-on accessory. Another design feature common to all Miuras was a functional louvered engine air scoop nestled behind each door window. The alloy wheel design persisted throughout the Miura's lifespan even as rim widths progressively increased. Raising the Miura's rear-hinged rear "clip" revealed Lamborghini's beautifully finished crosswise-mounted V-12 with individual throttle butterflies.

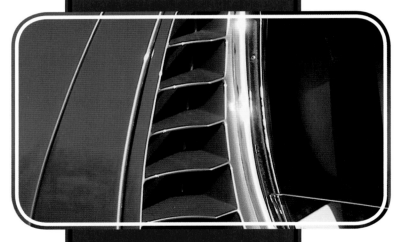

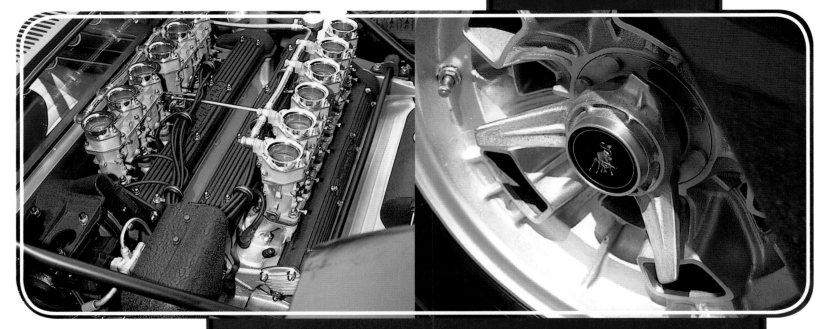

1972 LAMBORGHINI JARAMA AND 1972 P250

Replacing Lamborghini's front-engine Islero in 1970, the Jarama 400GT combined a shortened 93.5-inch-wheelbase version of the big Espada chassis with angular new Bertone bodywork by Marcello Gandini. But the Jarama ended up much heavier than the Islero, so in 1973 its 350-bhp 4.0-liter V-12 was up-tuned to 365 for a replacement 400GTS model, which sported a thin, wide hood scoop. But the Jarama never really impressed critics or buyers, and it was dropped in 1978 after just 327 were built.

Arriving in 1972, the 96.6-inch-wheelbase Lamborghini P250 Urraco was a sort of "baby Miura," with a similar mid-engine layout and chassis features but a single-cam 2.5-liter V-8 instead of a twin-cam V-12. The design was by Marcello Gandini, the body build by Bertone. To cope with the performance-sapping effects of multiplying U.S. regulations, a P300 model was added in 1974 with big black-rubber bumpers, evident here, but also a 3.0-liter twin-cam V-8 with 265 horsepower, up 45. Though agile, the Urraco had practical drawbacks that turned buyers off, and fewer than 780 were built through early 1979.

LAMBORGHINI COUNTACH

Designed by Bertone's Marcello Gandini (who had previously styled the gorgeous Miura), the four-wheeled spaceship that became the 1974 Countach ("coon-tash") was unveiled as the LP500 concept at the 1971 Geneva Motor Show…and was no less astonishing when it entered production to replace the Miura as the LP400 with "scissors" doors and a midship-mounted 370-hp 3.9-liter V-12. It was cramped, stiff-riding and difficult to see out of, but it was Batmobile cool and bat-outta-hell quick, capable of 175 mph and 0–60 in well under seven seconds.

That prototype's exterior was fine-tuned to reduce aerodynamic drag, improve high-speed stability and engine cooling and meet safety standards, then further refined through succeeding models leading to the 449-hp 25th Anniversary Edition. The LP400S debuted in 1978 with flared fenders, ultrawide wheels and tires, front spoiler, and refinements to suspension and cockpit. It wasn't faster but somewhat easier to drive in traffic, if one had to.

The few Americans fortunate enough to own a Countach did so mainly through "gray market" channels as Lamborghini's mounting financial troubles prevented it from meeting all U.S. standards. That made the Countach even more of a dream ride for folks with connections and over $50,000 to burn. A total of 1,983 Countaches were built during its 16-year lifetime.

1976 **LAMBORGHINI** SILHOUETTE

Unveiled in early 1976, the Lamborghini Silhouette was a semi-convertible based on the mid-engine Urraco coupe with flared, squared wheel arches and "five-hole" wheels. Everything else was the same.

managing a mere 50 or so Silhouettes through 1977. After that, the marque would be absent from the U.S. until 1983.

Cash-short Lamborghini hoped the new model would boost sales but could not afford to certify it for the U.S., where it might have sold best. This left would-be American buyers to deal with the gray market or one of the few private companies that would "federalize" a Euro model for a price. But it didn't matter anyway. Lamborghini couldn't build many cars of any kind in this period,

1970 LANCIA STRATOS HF ZERO

Italian coachbuilder Bertone took the wedge-shape, midengined sports car design to the limit with the 1970 Lancia Stratos HF Zero concept car. In spite of its extreme design, the Stratos was drivable with power provided by a Lancia V-4 engine. Passengers entered the Stratos by lifting the windshield. Lancia later built a more conventional production Stratos that did well in the World Rally Championship series.

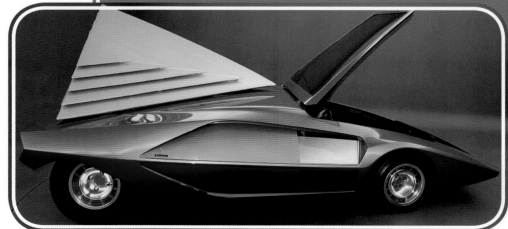

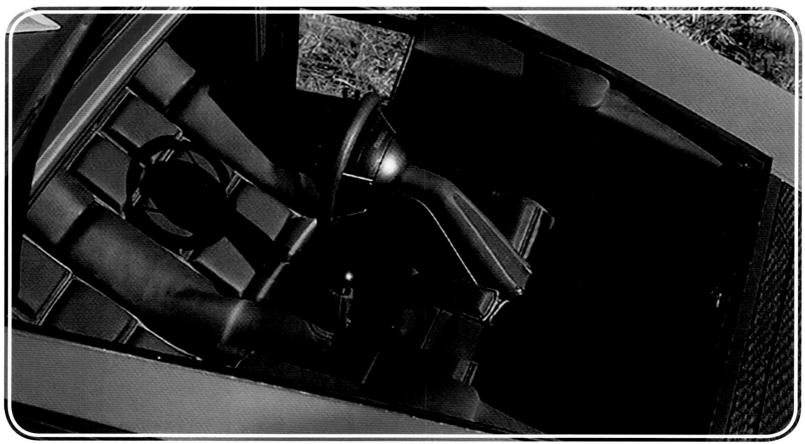

1970 LAND ROVER RANGE ROVER

The 1970 Land Rover Range Rover is credited with starting the SUV-as-status-symbol trend. Designed to be more quiet, comfortable and capable on-road than the rugged original Land Rover, the Range Rover's aluminum V-8 began as a Buick design. Rover bought its production tooling in the late 1960s, and it was capable of 100 mph top speed. Coil springs on all four corners helped provide a reasonably comfortable ride, yet its off-road abilities were retained so it could go almost anywhere. Rover thought the it would sell mostly to prosperous farmers and veterinarians, but these semi-luxury SUVs soon became common in London and other cities.

1970–79 LINCOLN
CONTINENTAL

For 1970, Lincoln introduced an all-new fifth-generation Continental two-door, four-door, and Town Car; the latter distinguished by a vinyl roof. Back on a body-on-frame structure (shared with Ford LTD and Mercury Marquis but with a longer wheelbase) after 13 years with unibody construction, it rode on coil springs at all four corners with front disc/rear drum brakes from 1970 to '74 and available

four-wheel discs from '75 to '79. A 460-cid V-8 was standard, but 1977 emissions standards brought a 400 V-8 for California that became standard (with the 460 optional) the following year. Then the 460 was dropped for 1979.

Following the downsizing of full-size GM and Chrysler cars, the 1977 Continental was the largest

mass-market automobile produced worldwide, surpassed only by purpose-built limousines, and five-mph bumpers made 1977–'79 Lincolns the longest cars ever produced by Ford Motor Company.

Continental's exterior was restyled with distinctive new rooflines for 1975. Two-door models adopted a fully pillared roofline with a square opera window in the C-pillar, four-door Continentals got a wide B-pillar, and Town Cars sported the oval opera window originally introduced on the Mark IV. Along with the styling upgrades, 1975 Lincolns boasted (industry rare) optional four-wheel disc brakes, and new catalytic converters required unleaded gasoline.

Another exterior revision came for 1977 with a narrower, Rolls-Royce-style grille nearly identical to that on the Mark V, and an optional fixed-glass moonroof with an interior sunshade was introduced as an alternative to the optional sliding glass sunroof.

1976 LOTUS ESPRIT

Lotus moved upmarket with its mid-'70s replacement for the mid-engine Europa. A wedgy, sharp-edged, two-seat coupe penned by Giorgetto Giugiaro, the Esprit followed Lotus tradition with a fiberglass body atop a steel "backbone" chassis on coil-spring/double-wishbone suspension. The engine was a new Lotus-developed 2.0-liter twin-cam four good for 140 bhp in initial U.S. tune.

An Esprit Turbo version launched overseas in 1980 with a turbo-charged 2.2-liter four, stiffer chassis, revised suspension and lower-body "aero" addenda, and it later came to America with 205 bhp, which delivered a Ferrari-like 6.6 sec. 0–60 mph and nearly 150 mph all out.

Regular or Turbo, the Esprit was one of the world's best-handling cars and, despite on-again/off-again U.S. sales, would be Lotus' chief money-earner into the early 21st century.

1971 MASERATI BORA

Maserati swelled the ranks of mid-engine production sports cars with its 1971 Bora. One of the first projects for designer Giorgetto Giugiaro's new Ital Design studio, the unibody two-seat fastback arrived with a 4.7-liter version of Maserati's familiar racing-derived twin-cam V-8 that sent 310 horsepower to the rear wheels via a manual five-speed transaxle. Rolling on a 102.2-inch wheelbase, the Bora used classic double-wishbone suspension, rack-and-pinion steering, and disc brakes with high-pressure hydraulics by Citroën of France, which had recently taken over Maserati and financed this new model. The hydraulics were also used for power-adjustable pedals, which combined with a tilt/telescope steering wheel for an unusually accommodating Italian cockpit. Tightening emissions requirements delayed U.S. sales until 1974, when a substitute 320-bhp 4.9-liter V-8 met that challenge. Though capable of 160 mph and 0–60 in just 6.5 seconds, the Bora was a civilized supercar. Yet it was pricey and rare. Interim changes were few, and just 571 were built through 1980.

1976 MASERATI MERAK SS

The Maserati Merak resembled the mid-V-8 Bora but carried a new Maserati-designed 3.0-liter twin-cam V-6 with 180 bhp in U.S. tune, which helped to enable a $5,000 lower price at about $22,000. Add-on "flying buttress" members mimicked the Bora's rear roof profile without its glass inserts, and a flat decklid replaced the Bora's lift-up hatch. Parent Citroën used the V-6 for its far-out SM coupe, while the Merak used the SM's dashboard.

U.S. sales began in late 1974, shortly before Alejandro DeTomaso took over Maserati. One result of that was the improved 1976 Merak SS, shown here, with discreet chin spoiler, wider

wheels and tires, Bora five-speed transaxle and conventional (non-Citroën) brakes and instrument panel. A good performer even in emissions-strangled U.S. form, the Merak would see modest production of 1,699 units through 1983.

1978 MAZDA RX-7

Hitting U.S. streets as a late 1978 model, the Mazda RX-7 was a new symbol for the growing success and influence of Japanese automakers. The small two-seat coupe combined conventional engineering with an unconventional engine: a compact Wankel rotary type producing 100 horsepower from just 1.2-liters of displacement. At around 2,500 pounds in U.S. trim, the RX-7 could run 0-60 mph in 9.7 seconds with its standard five-speed manual and was great fun on twisty back roads. "An enthusiast's dream come true," said one critic. It was well built, well equipped, and initially bargain priced at around $7,000. The RX-7 continued for six years with no basic design change, but it did get styling tweaks, added features and, for 1984, an upmarket GSL-SE model, shown here, with a 135-bhp 1.3-liter rotary.

1971 MERCEDES-BENZ SL

American-market tastes loomed large in the redesigned Mercedes-Benz SL launched in 1971. Compared to the W113 series of the 1960s, the new R107 was both longer and heavier. Its wheelbase grew to 96.7 inches, while curb weight ballooned to around 3,600 pounds as almost all body panels were steel rather than aluminum. But the result was also a stronger, quieter, and more refined two-seat Mercedes, which was just what the market wanted. The added heft was also deemed necessary to meet looming U.S. crash standards, but it required a larger, torquier engine to compensate.

The R107 bowed in Europe as the 350SL with a new 230-bhp 3.5-liter overhead-cam V-8. For easier compliance with U.S. emissions standards, Mercedes sent over a 450SL with a 4.5-liter V-8 but no more power. Euro models also wore single-lens headlamps, shown here, while the U.S. 450SL got a quartet of round sealed-beams that looked less tidy. But despite such compromises, lack of true sports-car agility and inevitably higher prices, the R107 sold like no SL before. The 450SL drew over 66,000 U.S. sales through 1980, after which the basic design soldiered on with a new engine as the 380SL.

1970 MERCURY CYCLONE GT AND CYCLONE SPOILER

Like its Ford Torino cousin, the Mercury Cyclone was redone for 1970, and the mid-size Mercs were 3.7 inches longer (on an inch-longer 117-inch wheelbase) and about 100 pounds heavier than their Ford counterparts. The Cyclone got a more conservative, semi-fastback roofline instead of the Torino's fastback SportsRoof. Standard interior equipment on Spoilers included high-back bucket seats and an Instrumentation Group that featured dash-mounted gauges angled toward the driver.

The mid-range Cyclone was the GT model with hidden headlamps and a 250-bhp 351 V-8 standard, but this prototype wears a GT grille badge that did not appear in production. The top performance Cyclone was the Spoiler, which—flaunting special graphics and spoilers front

and rear—was also the costliest model at $3,759. With 11.3:1 compression, Rochester Quadra-Jet carb and Ram Air induction, the standard 429 CJ pumped out 370 horsepower and a muscular 450 pound-feet of torque. Road Test's automatic with a 3.50:1 Traction-Lok rear axle ran a 14.61-sec. quarter mile at 99.22 mph.

1970 MERCURY COUGAR ELIMINATOR

Mercury's Cougar sport coupe got a new snout, and the Eliminator package entered its second and final year. The Mercury "Competition" hues matched Ford's "Grabber" colors, while standard Eliminator color choices were Pastel Blue or Competition Orange. The front spoiler may have worked aerodynamically, but Eliminator's rear spoiler was reportedly purely decorative, and the hood scoop was functional only with the 428 CJ.

1970 MERCURY COUGAR

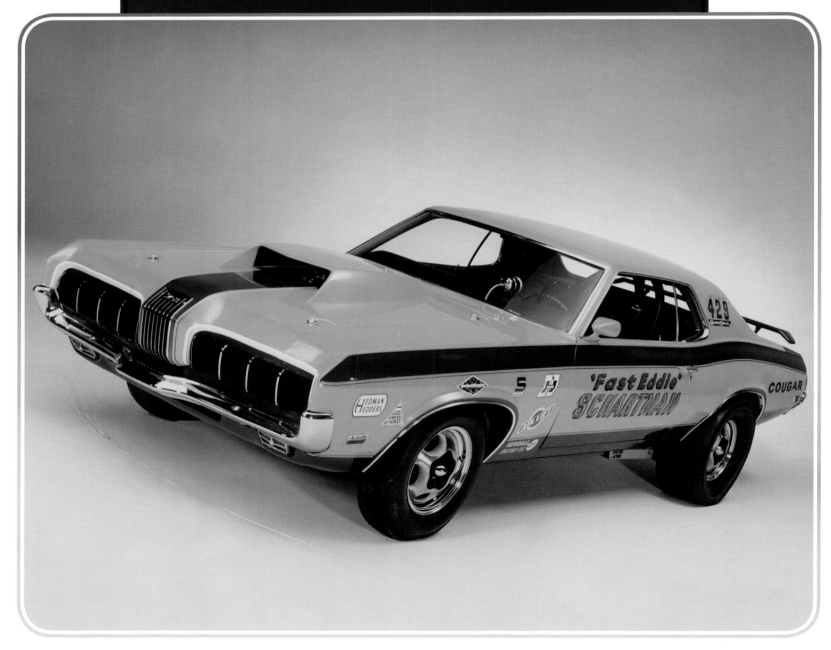

A 300-horsepower 351 was standard on the Cougar Eliminator, with the 290-bhp Boss 302 and 335-bhp 428 Cobra Jet optional, and Mercury dealers offered Autolite "Staged Performance" engine upgrade kits in three levels: Impressor, Controller, and Dominator. The Boss 429 V-8 was listed as a Cougar option, but only two are believed to have been installed. One was in "Fast" Eddie Schartman's drag car, seen here. Note the Lakewood "Traction Action" bars visible in front of the rear slicks. These "slapper bars" prevented excessive leaf spring flexing and helped prevent wheel hop for better traction.

1971 MERCURY CYCLONE SPOILER

The Cyclone Spoiler was back for 1971 with few changes beyond its new side stripes. Standard engine was a 285-horsepower 351 Cleveland, the 370-bhp 429 Cobra Jet was optional, and the 375-horse Super Cobra Jet also available too. Nevertheless, Cyclone sales plummeted from 13,496 units in 1970 to just 3,084 for '71, of which a mere 353 were Cyclone Spoilers.

1971 MERCURY COUGAR XR-7

Markedly bigger than before, the redesigned Mercury Cougar adopted a bulkier, more formal appearance. The Eliminator option was discontinued as muscle cars were beginning to be eclipsed in popularity by luxurious coupes, and the XR-7 sported chrome rocker-panel trim and a half-vinyl roof. Inside, its high-back buckets had leather seating surfaces. The top engine choice was a 429-cid V-8 that cranked out 370 horses.

1971 MERCURY MONTEGO GT

Mid-size Mercurys were remodeled along Torino lines for 1972. Cyclone was gone, leaving a new Montego GT fastback as the "muscle" model. Base price was $3,346 with the standard 302 V-8. The hottest power options included the 351 H.O. and big-block 429. Montego GT production was only 5,820 units, then Mercury pulled the plug on it after '73 sales fell to 4,464.

1974 MG MIDGET

Though the little Austin-Healey Sprite departed the market after 1971, its sister MG Midget soldered on until '74, when a revised Mark IV model appeared with rounded rear wheel arches, triple windshield wipers and other changes dictated by U.S. regulations. Besides an accessory luggage rack, this one wears five-spoke "Rostyle" steel wheels, a cheaper alternative to alloy rims.

The Midget returned to flat-top rear wheel arches for '75, but the big news was a 1,500cc four replacing the previous 1,275, which was being strangled by U.S. emissions limits. Also new were a jacked-up suspension and big, black, rubber bumpers to meet Washington's edict. But the bumpers and other added equipment increased weight, while the larger engine could manage just 50-62 horsepower in U.S. trim, about the same as the 1,275cc that preceded it.

Such halfhearted measures reflected growing financial trouble at parent British Leyland and an elderly design that was difficult to update. BL ladled on jazzy decals and "free extras" to keep buyers interested, and that helped for a while as Midget sales remained fairly healthy in the vital U.S. market. But this wasn't enough help for beleaguered BL, which reluctantly dropped the Midget after 1979. Over 86,000 Mark IV/1500s were sold, most of them in America.

1973 MGB

America missed out on the Rover-powered MGB GT V-8, which could do 125 mph but drew only 2,591 sales in 1973–76.

The MGB roadster halfheartedly met U.S. regulations with an elevated suspension, big 5-mph bumpers and just 62 emissions-strangled horsepower. Age, new competition, and rising prices conspired to end production for all markets in late 1980.

1978 MORGAN 4/4

Britain's Morgan offered its first four-wheeler, the 4/4, in 1935. A slightly larger, more powerful sports car, the Plus 4, replaced it in 1950, but the 4/4 returned five years later as a lower-priced four-cylinder Morgan. Like most every Morgan ever built, its body is a wood-frame, steel-paneled affair in nostalgic 1930s roadster form. Equally little-changed over time is the simple ladder-type chassis with underslung rear axle, very stiff springs and shock absorbers, and a sliding-pillar front suspension first used in 1910 on the company's three-wheeled car.

Morgan has always relied on engines from other car companies, subject to availability and price. This 4/4 carries a 1,600cc British Ford unit with 96 DIN horsepower, the sole choice from 1968 to 1982 and familiar in the U.S. in various Ford-built cars (and Formula Ford racers).

As expected of a "cottage industry" make like Morgan, the 4/4 evolved in step with the Plus 4 and its 1968 replacement, the V-8 Plus 8, which was soon followed by a four-seat 4/4. Morgan later moved to newer engines and revived the Plus 4, but the cars themselves still seemed as immutable as Gibraltar, which was fine with Morgan's customers, who kept coming back year after year for this unique blend of traditional sports-car character and modern componentry.

1970 OLDSMOBILE
CUTLASS W-31

Kooky Dr. Oldsmobile and his odd minions were still hamming it up in 1970 Oldsmobile performance-car advertising. But the prices of many high-end muscle cars were out of reach for many young enthusiasts, so automakers began offering more-affordable op-

tions that offered most of the "show" but not quite as much "go." The Oldsmobile Cutlass W-31 package brought many of the appearance and handling goodies of the 4-4-2 but packed a 325-bhp 350-cid small-block V-8 in place of the 4-4-2's thumping 455.

1970 OLDSMOBILE
CUTLASS 4-4-2 W-30

For 1970, Oldsmobile introduced perhaps the best all-around 4-4-2 ever. The major advance was the newly standard 455-cid big-block V-8, an under-stressed, big-port engine with tugboat torque. It made 365 bhp in base form, an underrated 370 in W-30 guise. A stylish facelift brought fresh front bumper and rear-bumper/taillight designs. The W-30 package included a fiberglass hood with functional scoops, plastic inner fenders, a rear-deck spoiler (which could be deleted) and less sound deadening than other 4-4-2s. Hardtop 4-4-2s started at $3,376.

1971 OLDSMOBILE
CUTLASS 4-4-2 W-30

Like all GM divisions, Oldsmobile detuned its engines for '71, but the 4-4-2 W-30 package still packed a factory-blueprinted 455-cid V-8 with the air-induction hood. However, under GM's net horsepower system (measuring output with all accessories in place), the base 455 was rated at just 260 horse-power and the W-30 at 300 bhp. The 4-4-2 came only as a $3,552 coupe weighing 3,688 pounds or a $3,743 convertible at 3,731 pounds. The W-30 package added $369. Both the W-32 and 350-cid W-31 packages were dropped for '71.

1971–78 OLDSMOBILE TORONADO

Oldsmobile's Toronado was most notable as GM's first front-wheel drive car and the first U.S.-built front-drive automobile since the 1930s Cord 810/812. The original 1966 model won several leading automotive awards, including *Motor Trend*'s Car of the Year and *Car Life*'s Award for Engineering Excellence.

Larger for 1971 and with heavily revised styling, the previous subframe design was replaced by body-on-frame construction similar to that of full-sized Delta 88 and Ninety-Eight models. The front torsion bar suspension was retained, but the rear multi-leaf springs were replaced by coil springs, front disc brakes became standard and rear-wheel ABS optional. In addition, a novelty (shared by Buick's Riviera) that later became

federally mandated were two high-mounted stop and turn-signal below the rear window.

The 455-cid Rocket V8 was carried over as standard, but implementation of a GM corporate edict that all engines had to run on low-lead fuel to meet increasingly tougher emission control regulations—a first

step toward introduction of catalytic converters in 1975—was met by lowered compression ratios and reduced output. Thus the 1971 Toronado's 455-cid V-8 was rated at 350 bhp, down from 375 in 1970. Nevertheless, Toronado sales increased dramatically. For 1972, the 455's rating dropped to 250 bhp thanks to a switch in power measurements from SAE gross to "net" ratings measured with all accessories and emissions equipment attached. By 1976, the last year for the 455 in the Toronado, its net rating had sunk to 215 hp.

The 1971–78 generation is also notable for an occupant safety first: from 1974–1976, it was part of GM's experimental production run of driver- and passenger-side "Air Cushion Restraint System" airbags. Other highlights include disc brakes with audible wear indicators for 1972, a federally mandated five-mph front bumper for 1973, a five-mph rear bumper

for '74 and rectangular headlights for '75. The later years of this generation saw mostly minor styling tweaks, although in 1977, XS and XSR models featured a three-sided, hot wire "bent-glass" rear window and, on the XSR, electric T-tops that slid inward at the touch of a button.

Also for 1977, the 455-cid V-8 was replaced by a smaller 403-cid engine rated at 185 bhp due mainly to forthcoming (1978) government Corporate Average Fuel Economy standards. In addition, all other GM full-size models were downsized, leaving the Toronado the largest Oldsmobile looking hopelessly out of place.

The 1979 third generation Toronado was substantially downsized, losing nearly 1,000 lb. and almost 16 in. in length, and powered by Oldsmobile's 350-cid V-8 rated at 170 bhp and 270 pound feet of torque.

1972 OLDSMOBILE NINETY-EIGHT REGENCY HARDTOP SEDAN

Both Oldsmobile and Cadillac celebrated anniversaries in 1972, Cadillac its 70th and Oldsmobile—then the oldest surviving American automaker—its 75th. And both decided to make it a velour anniversary. That fabric had vanished from car interiors after World War II, but thanks to the leads of Olds and Cadillac, it became the top upholstery choice for American cars in the 1970s.

Oldsmobile's velour seat had a pillowed effect that resembled a plush couch, a look that was widely copied during the '70s. This trendsetting interior made its debut in the Ninety-Eight Regency four-door hardtop, a mid-year model with a production run limited to 5,000 copies for '72. New York jeweler Tiffany & Co. styled the face of the Regency's dashboard clock and provided a sterling-silver key ring. Every Regency was painted Tiffany Gold metallic, but the interior was available in either black or gold.

Olds saw that it was onto a good thing and brought back the Regency as a regular model for '73, selling more than 34,000. The name would remain a part of the Ninety-Eight family until the end of that line in 1996, after which it transferred to the Eighty-Eight range through '98.

John Beltz, Oldsmobile's general manager from 1969 to 1972, said Olds buyers didn't want small cars, and at 228 inches long on a 127-inch wheelbase, the Ninety-Eight certainly wasn't.

Beltz also said it was much easier to reduce emissions from a big engine because it was usually operating at only part throttle. Of course, he said this before the 1973-74 OPEC oil embargo, when most Americans weren't yet overly concerned with fuel economy.

The Ninety-Eight's 250-bhp 455-cid V-8 move its 4,698 pounds quite well. A '71 Ninety-Eight did 0-60 mph in 8.7 seconds (but averaged only 11 mpg) in *Motor Trend* testing.

1972 OLDSMOBILE
4-4-2 W-30

Oldsmobile demoted the 4-4-2 to an appearance and handling option on select Cutlass models for 1972. The package included decal stripes and badging, plus the FE2 handling suspension with heavy-duty front and rear stabilizer bars, Hurst competition shifter, 14-inch wheels, louvered hood, and special 4-4-2 grille.

All automakers now reported net instead of gross horsepower and torque. The 4-4-2's standard engine was a 160-bhp 350-cid 2-bbl. V-8, a 180-hp 4-bbl. version was optional, as was a 4-bbl. 455 that made 250-bhp with the Turbo 400 automatic and 270 with the M20 four-speed manual. Top power option was still the $599 W-30 with a 300-bhp factory-blueprint-ed 4-bbl. 455 and a twin-scooped fiberglass Cold-Air Induction hood. Performance was still respectable: *Motor Trend*'s 4-4-2 W-30 did 0-60 in 6.6 seconds and the quarter mile in 14.5.

The last 4-4-2 convertibles were built this year, as the body style would not survive to '73. Total 4-4-2 production increased over '71 at 9,845 units, 772 of them W-30s. After testing the 1972 4-4-2, *Motor Trend* said, ". . . last year's compression drop was rather like hitting Dr. Oldsmobile with a malpractice suit. But there's still some soul left in Lansing, and despite all the furor, a 4-4-2 will still churn up all the smoke and fury the average muscle car driver could need and probably handle."

1973 OLDSMOBILE 4-4-2

Oldsmobile's Cutlass put its own stamp on GM's Colonnade body via unusual flared-out side character lines and a split grille that wrapped under the front bumper. The $121 4-4-2 package—available on base or Cutlass S coupes—added FE2 "Rallye" suspension, which consisted of heavy-duty stabilizer bars front and rear, beefier rear upper control arms, stouter springs, and 14-inch wheels. To look the part of a muscle car, 4-4-2s also got a louvered hood, bolder segmented grille, bodyside and hood/decklid stripes, and 4-4-2 badges. This Viking Blue example has the top Cutlass engine choice: a 250-bhp 4-bbl. 455-cid V-8.

1979 OLDSMOBILE HURST OLDS

The Hurst/Olds popped up again for 1979 on the recently downsized Cutlass Calais coupe. Its only available engine was a 170-bhp Olds-built 350 V-8 labeled "W-30" and linked to the THM-350 automatic with the traditional Hurst Dual-Gate shifter. All the H/O trimmings added $2,054 to the price of a Calais. Though arguably the least special Hurst/Olds, the '79 earned a reasonably warm reception with 2,499 built—1,165 mainly white, 1,334 primarily black. The gold two-toning was standard, T-tops optional and a power sunroof could be ordered.

1970 PLYMOUTH AAR 'CUDA

Of course, the street-going production AAR 'Cuda—named for Dan Gurney's All-American Racers, the team that campaigned Barracudas in the Sports Car Club of America's competition series—could not be mechanically identical to its Trans Am racing namesake. But unlike the Mustang Boss 302 and Camaro Z28 (both also were built to homologate race cars), it didn't even try to mimic the pavement-hugging posture of its competition cousins. What Plymouth decided to build instead was essentially a jacked-up street rod.

Like the similar racing Dodge Challenger T/As, track AARs ran full-race 440-bhp 305-cid four-barrel V-8s and were lowered and modified for twisty road-course combat. And like production Challenger T/As built to qualify the cars for racing, street AARs used a 290-bhp 340-cid with three 2-bbl. Holley carbs on an Edelbrock aluminum manifold breathing through a functional hood scoop. Buyers could choose a four-speed manual or TorqueFlite automatic with a Sure-Grip axle and standard 3.55:1 or optional 3.91:1 gears.

While the AAR's interior was basic 'Cuda, its exterior was not. From its matte-black fiberglass hood through body-side strobe stripes and tri-colored AAR shield to the standard black ducktail spoiler, this was an exotic fish. Special shocks and recambered rear springs raised the tail 1-3⁄4 inches, allowing clearance for exhaust pipes that exited in front of the rear wheel wells (after routing through the standard muffler beneath the trunk). It also permitted use of G60x15 tires in back and E60x15s in front. With a 56 percent front weight bias, handling was plagued by understeer, prompting *Car and Driver* to suggest "it might have been better to put the fat tires on the front wheels." But the AAR 'Cuda was strong in a straight line, and an eyeful anywhere.

1970 PLYMOUTH DUSTER 340

Just as it had with the Road Runner in 1968, Plymouth scored a budget-muscle bull's-eye in 1970 with the Duster 340. The formula was familiar: take a cheap-to-produce platform—in this case a Valiant wearing a new fastback body—and treat it to a hot engine, here a respected 340-cid 4-bbl. V8. Duster 340s offered an array of performance enhancers including heavy-duty underpinnings, front stabilizer bar, six-leaf rear springs and 14-in. tires on rally wheels. It borrowed the instrument panel from an earlier-series Barracuda, and bucket seats and a center console with floor shift could be ordered in place of the front bench. Starting at just $2,547, the lowest-price car in Plymouth's famed "Rapid Transit System," it was lighter, roomier, and quicker than the 340 Cuda—a true muscle-car bargain.

1970 PLYMOUTH
ROAD RUNNER

Plymouth's intermediate line finished its 1968–70 styling cycle with freshened sheetmetal, including loop-motif front and rear ends and dummy rear-fender scoops. Inside were a revised instrument panel and new available bucket seats. The engine lineup was unchanged with the 440 Six Barrel V-8 again an option, but a heavy-duty three-speed manual became the standard transmission, relegating the four-speed to the options list along with the Torque-Flite automatic. Sales of the 1970 Road Runner dropped by more than 50 percent over the previous year to around 41,000 units (about 1,000 ahead of Pontiac's GTO but some 13,000 behind Chevy's Chevelle SS-396/454). This was the second and last year for the Road Runner convertible with just 834 built, of which only three were powered by the Hemi R-code V-8.

1970 PLYMOUTH HEMI 'CUDA

Many agreed that the redesigned 1970 Barracuda was one of the prettiest pony cars of its day, and Hemi 'Cuda versions were among the most potent. The Barracuda looked lean, and with the right engine, it could also be very mean. The sporting' 'Cuda derivations featured a wide choice of five V-8 engines, from the 275-bhp 340 and 335-bhp 383 to the 375-bhp four-barrel 440, the 390-bhp 440+6 and the 425-bhp 426 Hemi, the latter now with hydraulic lifters. The 440 and Hemi versions got a suspension tailored to heavy-metal acceleration with no stabilizer bar in back, five right-side leaf springs and six on the left, with thicknesses chosen to equalize tire loads under hard acceleration. Total 1970 'Cuda production numbered 17,792 of which 652 hardtops and just 14 convertibles were Hemi-powered.

SHAKER

1970 PLYMOUTH
ROAD RUNNER SUPERBIRD

Aerodynamic testing began to come into its own in automotive design in the late 1960s. Cars of all sorts benefited, but few had the visual drama of the Plymouth Road Runner Superbird.

Like its Dodge cousin, the '69 Charger Daytona, the Superbird was a "homologation special": To be eligible to run in NASCAR events in 1970, a given model's production run had to equal half the number of the manufacturer's dealers, or 1,000 cars, whichever was higher. Ultimately, 1,920 Superbirds were made and offered for sale at steep prices that began at $4,298.

The metal front-nose clip, with chin spoiler and fiberglass tubs for pop-up headlamps, was fitted to front fenders and a lengthened hood borrowed from the '70 Dodge Coronet. Other aerodynamic parts, including the towering aluminum wing, were developed expressly for the Belvedere/Road Runner body so were unrelated to similar pieces om the Charger Daytona. Also unique were the Warner Bros. Road Runner graphics, which gave this very serious competition car a nice touch of whimsy. All production Superbirds wore vinyl tops that hid the weld seams left by installation of the flush-mounted back window. As on the Charger Daytona, rearward-facing scoops on the front fenders were nonfunctional on production Superbirds but allowed the fender tops to be cut for tire clearance and suspension travel on competition cars.

Three engines were offered: a 375-bhp 440 with a single 4-bbl. carburetor, the 390-bhp 440 Six Pack with triple 2-bbl. carbs, or the

425-horse 426 Hemi with a 10.25:1 compression ratio.

In competition trim, the Superbird could top 220 mph; at the 1970 Daytona 500, Pete Hamilton beat the field with an average speed of 150 mph, and the Superbird went on to take 21 of 38 Grand National events that year.

1971 PLYMOUTH ROAD RUNNER

Plymouth's "Rapid Transit System" continued in 1971 with a radically restyled Road Runner. Wheelbase dropped an inch to 115, the rear track was three inches wider for better handling, the interior was reconfigured, and the only body style was a hardtop coupe. Although Chrysler Corp. was slowest of Detroit's Big Three to scale back on horsepower, not all of its V-8s escaped detuning. While the seldom-ordered 426 Hemi held fast at 425 bhp, Road Runner's standard 383-cid 4-bbl. V-8 was down 35 bhp to 300, and its optional triple-2-bbl. 440+6 lost five ponies to 385. During the year, a 275-bhp "small-block" 340 V8 was also made available. Options included a body-color elastomeric front bumper, an Air Grabber hood with a pop-up scoop and a trunk-mounted rear spoiler. With rising insurance rates and tougher emissions standards sapping muscle cars' appeal, buyers who ponied up the Road Runner's $3,147 starting price enjoyed one of the last true performance machines of the era.

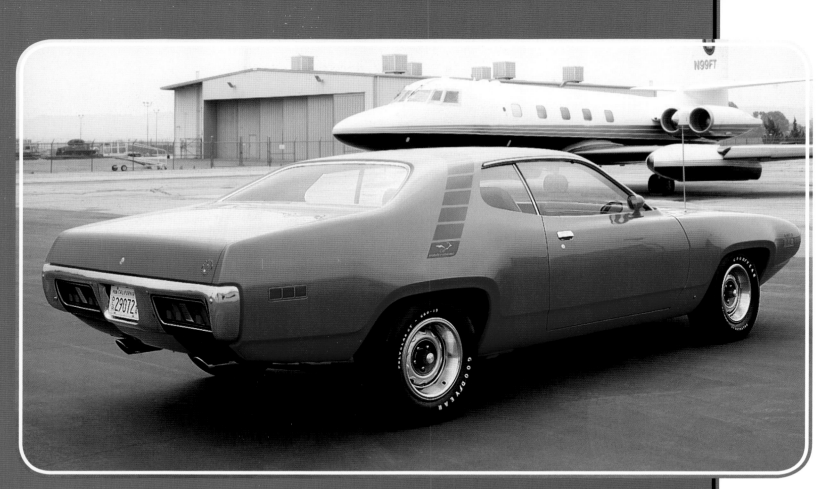

1971 PLYMOUTH 'CUDA

While some 'Cuda rivals dialed back on performance to appease emissions and insurance concerns, Plymouth still offered a broad muscle-car range. As seen on this 440 6-bbl. convertible, the functional shaker scoop—standard on Hemis, optional on other engines—mounted directly to the air cleaner and shook through a hole in the hood as the engine rocked.

1971 PLYMOUTH HEMI 'CUDA

Of the total 1971 Barracuda production of 18,690, convertibles accounted for just 1,388, a mere 374 of those were 'Cudas, and just 11 were optioned with the 425-bhp 426 Hemi V-8. Historians originally believed that total was nine but later learned that two additional Hemi 'Cuda convertibles had been exported to France. This Winchester Gray metallic example is one of those French cars. It has a four-speed manual; the other was an automatic.

1973 PLYMOUTH BARRACUDA

Plymouth's Barracuda changed little for 1973. Base cars offered a standard 318-cid V-8 instead of their previous 225-cid slant six, and 'Cudas still came with the 340 V-8 and dual-scooped hood. With start-ing stickers of $2,935 for Barracuda and $3,120 for 'Cuda, production increased to 22,213, of which a bit more than half (11,587) were base Barracudas.

1973 PLYMOUTH DUSTER

Duster got a handsome facelift for 1973, and its variants proliferated. A luxury package made Duster a Gold Duster, addition of an optional sunroof and a fold-down rear seat made it into a Space Duster, and the Duster 340 packed 240 bhp. Duster production was 249,243 for 1973, and the Duster 340 sold 15,731 units. With muscle fading fast, some performance dealers offered high-performance specials. Mr. Norm's Grand-Spaulding Dodge of Chicago developed a GSS Supercharger kit for the 1972 Demon, and this 1973 Duster has that blower setup.

1973 PLYMOUTH
ROAD RUNNER

For 1973, Plymouth's Road Runner was still running, in name if not in spirit, at a time when other hot cars were dropping like . . . well, the famous cartoon's old Wile E. Coyote. Its restyle was chunky but handsome, with big rubber bumper guards helping meet new government standards. Under its bulged hood was a 170-bhp 2-bbl. 318 V-8 as its new standard engine.

Though performance wasn't close even to 1971 levels, some Mopar muscle was still available. The 340 V-8 delivered 240 horsepower, a 400 brought 255 ponies, and the big 440 soldiered on at 280 bhp, and both 340 and 400 engines could be backed by a four-speed manual gearbox with a Hurst pistol-grip

shifter. Reduced competition and a still-reasonable $3,095 starting sticker help explain why Road Runner sales recovered to 19,056.

1974 PLYMOUTH 'CUDA

Entering its final (Gen I) year in 1974, Barracuda's only major change was the 245-bhp 360-cid V-8 replacing the 340 as standard on 'Cuda and a $259 option on base cars. Mopar enthusiasts knew the 360 was not designed for high performance, but it could move. As time ran out, just 11,734 '74 Barracudas were built, an ignominious end.

1974 PLYMOUTH DUSTER

Duster remained the most popular Plymouth for 1974, and the sunroof and fold-down rear seat mark this one as a Space Duster. This package was Plymouth's response to compact hatchbacks like the AMC Hornet and Chevy Nova, while the performance model became Duster 360 thanks to its new 360-cid engine.

1975 PLYMOUTH ROAD RUNNER

Plymouth unveiled a redesigned and renamed range of mid-sizers for 1975. The Satellite moniker was replaced by the Fury name, moved down from the full-size cars, which were renamed Gran Fury, and Road Runner was an option on the base Fury coupe. Some saw the blocky styling as a snooze, along with the standard 318 V-8 backed by a three-speed stick. The four-speed and the 440 were history, leaving a 235-horse 400 as the top engine option.

1977 PLYMOUTH VOLARE ROAD RUNNER SUPER PAK

After a year as a Fury option, Road Runner migrated to the compact Volaré for '76. Then for '77, it was top of the heap of the two-door Volarés the marketing types called the "Fun Runners." Good for 150 horses, its standard 318 could be mated to three- or four-speed manuals or the TorqueFlite automatic. Still at 175 ponies, the 360 came only with automatic. The Super Pak option added front and rear spoilers, wheel flares, and quarter-window louvers.

1978 PLYMOUTH VOLARE ROAD RUNNER AND SUPER COUPE

Volaré was lightly facelifted for 1978 with a new grille and taillamps. Road Runners wore revised bright-colored striping, and the Sport Pack added spoilers, flares, and revised quarter-window louvers. The Super Coupe's stripes were brighter and body colors different, but Plymouth's execution was otherwise nearly the same as Dodge's. Fewer than 500 were made.

1971 PLYMOUTH HEMI 'CUDA

Volaré coupe buyers were offered a "Street Kit Car" option package—inspired by the build-it-yourself "Kit Car" short-track kit prepared in Richard Petty's race shop and sold through Chrysler—for $1,085. The two-tone blue street version added bolt-on fender flares, a big rear spoiler, metal window straps, and large "43" (Richard Petty's race number) graphics on the roof and doors. Dodge offered a Street Kit Car Aspen that looked nearly the same except for two-tone red paint. Plymouth reportedly sold 247 Street Kit Cars, and Dodge moved about 145.

1970 PONTIAC CATALINA

Pontiac became a force to be reckoned with during the 1960s with bold, exciting cars, and by 1970, that boldness was exemplified in its large cars. Unfortunately, big and brawny was falling out of favor, and

sales would suffer. The face of the 1970 full-sized Pontiacs harkened back to the classic era with a narrow vertical grille and a thin biplane-style bumper. Low-line Catalinas and all wagons rode a 122-inch wheelbase, Executives and Bonnevilles a 125-inch span. Pontiac's former 428-cid V-8 was bored and stroked to become a 455 for 1970. Standard in Bonnevilles and optional in the other full sizers, this new top-dog V-8 came in 360- and 370-horse flavors. The Catalina convertible started at $3,604, and only 3686 were made.

1970 PONTIAC FIREBIRD TRANS AM

Firebird and Camaro grew more European in character with their second-generation redesign, but the scooped and spoiled Trans Am was pure American muscle, and its standard 345-bhp 400-cid Ram Air V-8 delivered low-14-second quarter-mile ETs. That satisfied most buyers, because just 88 of 3,196 Trans Ams built for '70 got the optional Ram Air IV, which added bigger ports, better heads, swirl-polished valves and an aluminum intake manifold for 370 bhp, 25 more than in '69. Rarer still was the Ram Air V, a special-order piece with solid lifters and

tunnel-port heads for as much as 500 bhp. All these engines breathed through a new rear-facing shaker scoop designed to capture cool ambient air flowing

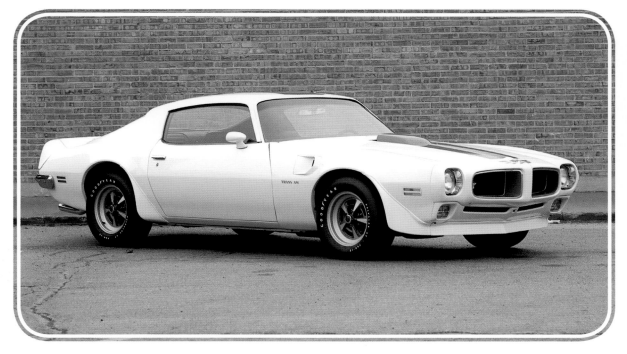

over the hood. A four-speed manual with Hurst shifter was standard, a Turbo Hydra-Matic optional. Both came with a 3.55:1 rear axle, and a 3.73:1 was available with the four-speed.

The padded Formula steering wheel directed quick 12.1:1 variable-ratio power steering while stiffer springs and heavy-duty sway bars front and rear teamed with F60x15 Polyglas tires on Rally II wheels and standard 10.9-inch power front disc brakes and 9.5-inch rear drums. Trans Ams wore the same impact-absorbing snout as other Firebirds, but Pontiac said its unique front air dam and fender air extractors created 50 pounds of downforce on the nose at expressway speeds, and that a big decklid lip and small spoilers ahead of the rear wheels gave equal downforce at the rear. Inside, the standard complete instrumentation included a racer-style tachometer turned on its side to redline at 12 o'clock. Even with 57 percent of its weight on the front wheels, *Sports Car Graphic* said, "Overall handling feel—for a production car—was as near to a front-engine race car as we have ever driven." *Car and Driver* called the '70 Trans Am "a hard muscled, lightning-reflexed commando of a car, the likes of which doesn't exist anywhere in the world, even for twice the price."

1970 PONTIAC FIREBIRD FORMULA 400

With the second-generation redesign that appeared in late February 1970, the scooped and spoilered Trans Am was pure American muscle and more immodest than ever. But the tamer Formula 400 shed the Trans Am's spoilers and swapped its "shaker" hood for a twin-scooped fiberglass unit. It came with a 330-bhp 400, and the scoops were functional when Ram Air was ordered. These Gen II Firebirds were all fastback coupes with no convertible available.

1970
PONTIAC
TEMPEST GT-37

The styling of all mid-size Pontiacs was significantly updated for 1970. The Tempest, LeMans, and LeMans Sport received a new front bumper/grille design that bore a passing resemblance to the 1969 Firebird. Sculpted bodysides featured character lines that flared out above the wheels, and the rear bumper was redesigned to house wraparound taillamps. Pontiac issued a mid-year "budget performance" GT-37 package that added a Hurst-shifted three-speed, hood-lock pins, Rally II wheels on F70x14 white-letter tires, dual exhausts with rear-valance tips, GT-37 badges, and '69 Judge-style stripes to V-8 Tempest coupes and hardtop coupes.

1970 PONTIAC GTO

The 1970 GTOs received a new all-Endura nose with twin grille openings; disappearing headlamps were no longer offered. But the big news was under the hood: an available 455-cid V-8 rated at 360 bhp, or 370 with the standard three-speed manual. It joined the carried-over 400, which made 350 bhp in standard tune, 366 with Ram Air III, and 370 with Ram Air IV. This GTO convertible wears redline tires, but most muscle cars by then had switched to raised-white-letter tires as factory equipment. The GTO's popularity was starting to slip; and 1970 convertible production was just 3,783 cars.

1970 PONTIAC GTO JUDGE

Pontiac altered the GTO's styling for 1970, giving it a new "Endura" nose with exposed headlamps, sharp bodyside creases, and a revised rear end. Under-hood, a newly optional 360-bhp 455 V-8 provided a muscular 500 pound-feet of torque at just 3,100 rpm, perfect for the option-laden luxury tourers many Goats had become. Pontiac kept the Judge focused on performance, and the 455 was kept off the docket until the last quarter of the model year. Most Judges packed the 366-horse 400-cid Ram Air III, but a handful had the extra-cost Ram Air IV with 370 ponies. Few cars made a bolder visual statement. "The Judge" decals returned, multi-hued stripes appeared over the bodyside creases, and the 60-inch rear wing now stood high and proud on the tail.

1971 PONTIAC GRAND VILLE

Pontiac had an all-new series of big cars for 1971. Catalina was still the low-end model, but Bonneville was demoted to mid-line status. The top-of-the-line series for '71 was the Grand Ville. The Grand Ville—offered in two- and four-door hardtop styles, along with a convertible—was the closest Pontiac would ever get to having GM's prestigious "C" body return to its lineup. Based on the "B" body, Grand

Villes borrowed formal hardtop rooflines from the new C-body Cadillac, Buick Electra, and Oldsmobile Ninety-Eight. This clever parts swapping gave Pontiac a new premium series and kept costs manageable. Grand Villes used the four-barrel version of the 455 that was optional on the other full-size models. The $4706 Grand Ville convertible sold 1789 copies.

1971 PONTIAC LEMANS SPORT

Pontiac's mid-size line was facelifted for 1971, and the Tempest name was retired. Base cars became T-37s, then came LeMans, LeMans Sport, and GTO in ascending order. All wore restyled front ends, and the GTO got a new hood. When equipped with an optional V-8 engine, T-37 coupe and hardtop coupe models could be turned into "budget GTO" GT-37s. The GT-37 package included dual exhausts, floor-mounted heavy-duty three-speed manual transmission, G70-14 white-letter tires on Judge-style Rally II wheels, hood pins, vinyl body stripes, and specific badging. LeMans Sport models, like the convertible shown, were available with an Endura option that added the new body-color front bumper, hood and headlamp surrounds.

1971 PONTIAC GT-37

Pontiac's entry-level mid-size lineup lost its Tempest nameplate in favor of the T-37 moniker, and a GT-37 package was targeted at performance-minded but cash-strapped buyers. Available with the 2-bbl. 350 V-8, the 4-bbl 400 or the 4-bbl. 455, it included the same basic dress-up equipment as in 1970 with the addition of some new bodyside stripes. Pontiac's 1971 catalog claimed, "There's a little GTO in every GT-37, and you don't have to be over 30 to afford it!" But the GT-37 never caught on with buyers, and the package was dropped after a minuscule 1971 production run.

1971 PONTIAC FIREBIRD TRANS AM AND FORMULA

Firebird changed little for 1971 after its strike-shortened 1970 model year, though Formula 350 and 455 models joined the Formula 400. While Trans Ams sported "look-at-me" scoops, spoilers, and paint, the Formula models' clean, unadorned shape also made a strong statement, and louvered vents behind the front wheels were a new touch on all Firebirds except Trans Am. In anticipation of new federal emissions standards just around the corner, all GM engines were required to run on unleaded fuel, yet Trans Ams still packed a strong, new, 335-bhp 455 HO V-8. Perhaps partly because this engine was also offered in the cheaper Formula, model year sales of the $4,590 T/A fell to just 2,116.

1971 PONTIAC
GTO AND GTO JUDGE

Pontiac's potent Ram Air engines were discontinued this year as GM lowered compression ratios to allow the use of unleaded fuel. The '71 455 HO had fewer horses than the previous optional Ram Air IV 400, yet it pumped out more torque at lower rpm and was better behaved on the street than the high-strung 400 IV. This Tropic Green ragtop is one of only 17 Judge convertibles built. Optional "honeycomb" wheels offered a distinctive appearance on Pontiac performance cars but added weight due to their heavy polyurethane/steel construction.

GTOs got a new hood and front fascia for 1971, and Judges came standard with the top available GTO engine, the 335-bhp 455 HO. The Judge ran the quarter in 14.9 sec. for *Motor Trend* compared to 15.4 sec. for a 300-bhp 400-cid GTO. Zero-60 times were 7.0 for the Judge vs. 7.1 for the Goat—both equipped with four-speed manuals and 3.55:1 rear axles. Insurance rates and changing tastes caused total GTO production to dwindle to 10,532, and the Judge was retired in mid-1971 after just 374 were built.

1972 FIREBIRD FORMULA

The 1972 Firebirds were visually unchanged save for the deletion of 1971's front-fender vents and a honeycomb mesh grille insert that nicely matched the available honeycomb wheels. The '72 Formula 400 stickered at a fairly affordable $3,221, but just 5,250 Formulas were sold as Firebird sales continued to nosedive. With total output plummeting 44 percent, the entire Firebird line ended the year in danger of cancelation.

1972 PONTIAC FIREBIRD TRANS AM

Trans Ams continued as racy as ever, and the price was cut $340 to $4,256 in hopes of sparking sales. But the public's continued drift away from performance combined with a factory strike held T/A production to just 1,286 for the model year. Trans Am's shaker-hood 455 returned with 300 net horsepower, down from 1971's 335 gross. And torque also fell. A four- speed manual transmission replaced a three-speed as standard. *Car and Driver* ran one with 3.42:1 gearing to 60 mph in just 5.4 seconds and through the quarter at 13.9 at 104.6 mph.

1972 PONTIAC GTO

Because performance wasn't selling like it had a few years earlier, and "personal" luxury was sought by more and more buyers, Pontiac added two-door and four-door hardtop Luxury LeMans models to its mid-size lineup. Exterior differences included a specific grille, trim, wheel covers, rear fender skirts, and badges, while interior upgrades included simulated Ceylonese teak trim, extra sound insulation, and all-Morrokide or patterned cloth/Morrokide upholstery. On the other end of the mid-size spectrum, the GTO was now a $344 option package on LeMans two-door coupes and hardtops, and the little-ordered Judge and convertible were retired. GTO appearance was little changed except for a revised grille and new front-fender vents.

1972 PONTIAC GRAND PRIX HURST SSJ

Pontiac's popular Grand Prix "personal" coupe was updated for 1971 with a new, less-pointy vertical grille and two headlamps replacing quads, plus a boat-tail-style rear deck. GP was largely the same for 1972 except for a fresh grille texture, a maintenance-free battery, and a handful of additional tweaks. Of particular interest was the limited-production Hurst SSJ Grand Prix that was first offered in 1970. Based on a Cameo White or Starlight Black Model J, this $1,147 conversion was done in a Hurst facility with special touches including Hurst's distinctive Firefrost Gold paint on the hood, roof and rear deck, Rally II wheels, a landau-style vinyl top, and an electrically operated steel sunroof.

1973 PONTIAC GTO

The once mighty GTO was fading by 1973 but remained an option package for the redesigned base and Sport LeMans coupe. Its only visual distinctions were a NACA-scooped hood, black grilles, specific badging, and—despite its healthy 400-cid V-8 and heavy-duty three-speed floor-shift transmission—it was less convincing than GTOs of just a few years before.

Pontiac's big news on the mid-size front was the new Grand Am, clearly related to LeMans but different enough to merit separate-series status. The mission of this coupe and sedan was Grand Prix comfort and luxury with Firebird Trans Am handling, and critics hailed it as the best-handling Detroit car of its time. Still, the public bought only about 43,000 copies.

1973 PONTIAC TRANS AM

The 1973 Trans Am introduced "Radial Tuned Suspension," which rolled on 15-inch radial tires said to deliver a more comfortable ride as well as better cornering. It also had to meet new safety and emissions requirements plus a beefed-up five-mph front bumper with extra steel reinforcements and core support to the fenders. And it added two new colors, Buccaneer Red and Brewster Green, and an updated hood bird, a $55 option that nearly every buyer ordered. Its standard 455 V-8 was rated at 250 bhp and 370 pound-feet of torque, while the "hand-assembled" LS2 SD-455 delivered 290 bhp and 395 pound-feet. All Pontiac engines included a new EGR system, which delayed the SD-455 program until late in the year. Trans Am production was up at 4,802, 252 with the SD-455, 72 of those with the manual transmission.

1974 PONTIAC GTO

The name was the same, but the image and most of the performance were gone. Based on the ho-hum Ventura compact—a Chevrolet Nova clone—the once-mighty GTO was a mere shadow of itself by 1974. Two pillared coupe body styles were available, one with a traditional trunk, the other with a hatchback that opened to a cargo area that could be enlarged by folding down the rear seat.

Only 7,058 units were built that year with the $195 GTO option package, which included a distinctive grille, a "shaker" hood scoop and a 350-cid V-8 rated at 200 horsepower. Purists bemoaned these emasculated 1974 GTOs, recalling the days when those three letters had stood for truly muscular performance. So GTO vanished into Pontiac history after 1974 until it reappeared in 2004 on a high-performance coupe built by GM Holden in Australia.

1974 PONTIAC TRANS AM

For 1974, Pontiac's Firebird was deftly restyled to accommodate federal five-mph bumpers without ruffling its great-looking feathers. The clever facelift added a soft "shovel-nose" Endura front end with Pontiac's traditional split grille as well as larger tail-lamps in back. Base, Esprit, Formula, and Trans Am models were available, and the big news was a re-surgence of the Trans Am. The standard V-8 became a 225-bhp 400-cid job, and a 290-horse Super Duty 455 was optional. The latter was rare, appearing in only 943 cars, 212 of them with stick shift. Surpris-ingly, in light of higher fuel prices resulting from the OPEC oil embargo, sales spurted upward in 1974. A total of 73,729 Firebirds were built, including a record 10,225 Trans Ams.

1975 PONTIAC GRAND VILLE BROUGHAM

Pontiac's full-size line evolved a bit each year during the first half of the 1970s, and this constant tweaking kept the cars reasonably fresh. Visual changes for 1975 included new rooflines for nearly all closed models except station wagons, and rectangular quad head-lamps—a new trend for upper-level GM cars—were found on Bonnevilles and Grand Villes.

In addition, the 1975 model year marked the debut of catalytic converters in most models, which required unleaded fuel. Also, the convertible body style made its final appearance in Pontiac's full-size line when a total of 4,519 Grand Ville Brougham droptops were sold.

1976 PONTIAC FIREBIRD FORMULA

The 1976 Firebird Formula boasted a new appearance package with bold FORMULA graphics along the lower body. Incorporated into a full-length, blacked-out strip, this suggestion of serious intent enhanced the mid-range model's attraction for customers who didn't need (or couldn't afford) a Trans Am. The Formula also got a new hood with twin hood scoops set further back than before. Pontiac made a point of promoting a Formula painted Goldenrod Yellow with black lower-body striping in its ads, but the special Keystone Rogue aftermarket wheels seen on this prototype were not a regular production option.

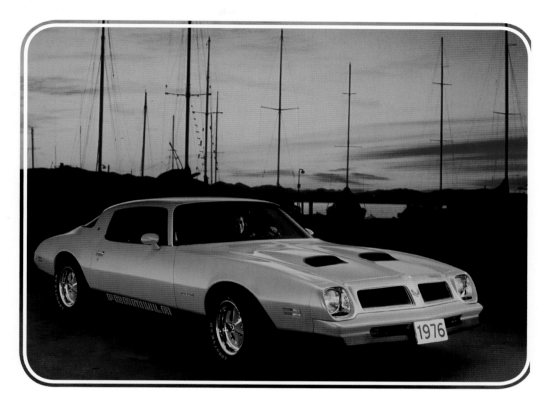

1976 PONTIAC TRANS AM

Trans Am lost its 455-cid V-8 for 1975, regained it for '76, then dropped it for good after that.

Base price for this '76 T/A was $4,987, and the 455 was a $150 option. This top engine provided decent performance, with *Motor Trend* recording low-16-sec. ETs and a 120-mph top speed for its test '76 455 T/A. Sales steadily grew as Trans Am's rivals disappeared: 46,701 T/As were built for '76, 68,745 for '77, and 93,341 for '78.

1977 PONTIAC GRAND PRIX

Like all GM intermediates, Pontiac's Grand Prix was redesigned for 1973. Its wheelbase shrunk two inches to 116, and its new body was shared with Chevrolet, Oldsmobile, and Buick. Luxury coupes were very popular during the mid- and late-1970s, and Grand Prix found more than 288,000 buyers—the best year ever for GP sales, and the last before it was dramatically downsized for 1978. All three 1977 trim levels—base, SJ, and LJ—had full model status, and the base car was most popular with 168,247 assembles. Standard engine was a new 301-cubic-inch Pontiac V-8 good for 135 horsepower. The line-topping LJ started at $5,753, but the sticker's bottom line could top $9,000 if every option was ordered.

1977 PONTIAC CAN AM

1977 was four years after the last real GTO and the last year before all GM intermediates would be downsized. And in the narrow window between the 1973 and '79 fuel crises, Pontiac reinjected some performance into its LeMans line. This "Limited Edition" LeMans Sport Coupe aggressively renamed "Can Am" combined beefier running gear with the Trans Am's 200-horse 400-cid V-8 (California and high-altitude models settled for an Oldsmobile-sourced 185-bhp 403), a "shaker" hood scoop, a rear spoiler, and decals. Also included in the $5,419 base price were power front disc brakes, variable-ratio power steering, front and rear stabilizers, and Pontiac's RTS handling package on GR70-15 steel-belted radials. All wore Cameo White paint with red/orange/yellow trim and a Grand Prix-style dash.

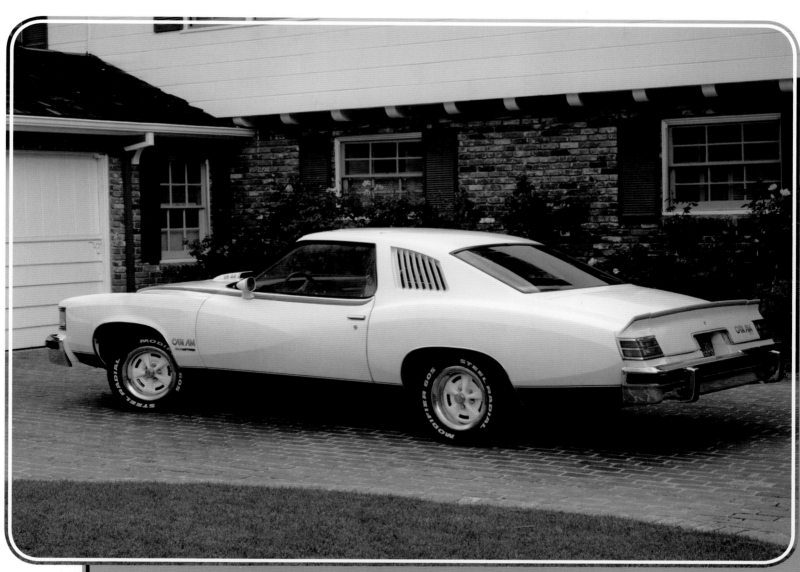

1977 PONTIAC
FIREBIRD TRANS AM

Pontiac's clever stylists were good at periodically imparting refreshing new looks to the Firebird without serious body modifications, and buyers were offered a new pointed snout with quad headlights set in a split grille for 1977. The 455 was gone, leaving a 400-cid V-8 for the Trans Am—except for California and high-altitude cars, which for emissions reasons got an Olds-built 403 V-8 instead. Inspired by the

similarly decorated '76 Trans Am that celebrated Pontiac's 50th anniversary, this gold-on-black "Special Edition" proved highly popular thanks largely to the one that played a central role in the 1977 *Smokey and the Bandit* movie. Trans Am sales totaled 68,745 for the year, including 15,567 of these gold-on-black beauties.

1978 PONTIAC GRAND AM

Pontiac's Grand Am had two three-year runs in the 1970s: 1973–75 and 1978–80 before being canceled and its spot in the lineup filled in 1982 by the Pontiac 6000. While the '73–'75 version was based on GM's mid-size A-body architecture, the rebirthed 1978 Grand Am shared the smaller LeMans/Grand Prix G-body platform. Offered in both two- and four-door models, they sported a vertical bar grille and other trimmings to differentiate them from LeMans models.

Like the sporty 1973–75 Grand Ams, this new generation featured "Radial Tuned Suspension" with front and rear sway bars on standard radial tires. And similar to their Grand LeMans cousins, their interiors offered a standard notchback front bench seat, optional 60/40 bench or Strato bucket seats with console and passenger-side recliner, a choice of cloth or Morrokide vinyl upholstery and full instrumentation with an optional tachometer.

Power steering, power front disc brakes, Turbo Hydramatic transmission and Pontiac's 140-bhp 301-cid (4.9-liter) 2-bbl. V-8 were standard, while a 155-bhp 4-bbl. version of the 301 V-8, snowflake wheels, whitewall or white-lettered tires, power windows and seats, tilt steering wheel, sunroof and cruise control were optional. Due to tougher emissions requirements, California cars offered a choice of 135-bhp 2-bbl. or 145-bhp 4-bbl. 305-cid Chevrolet V-8s.

Changes were few for 1979 except that the standard Grand Am powertrain devolved to a 231- cid (Buick) V-6 driving through a floor-mounted three-speed manual transmission while both 301 V-8s and the Turbo Hydramatic became optional. But the 49-state 301 4-bbl. was uprated to 150 bhp and could be coupled to an available four-speed manual gearbox. Then for 1980, the four-door Grand Am was dropped along with the V-6 and 2-bbl. V-8s, leaving just the 4-bbl. 301 (uprated again to 170 bhp) in 49 states and a 160-bhp 305-cid Chevy V-8 in California.

1979 PONTIAC
10TH ANNIVERSARY TRANS AM

Firebirds were facelifted for 1979 with a new front fascia and separate quad headlamps inset above twin grille openings in the bumper. On Trans Ams and Formulas, a new full-width taillight panel featured a smoked-glass look that glowed red when illuminated. But that year's big news was the fully loaded 10th Anniversary Trans Am wearing two-tone silver and charcoal paint, a super-bird hood decal that flowed into the fenders, and special emblems and striping. It also boasted a T-bar roof with silver-tint glass hatches, the WS-6 handling package, and a custom silver leather interior with shag car-

peting, a leather-wrapped Formula steering wheel and red instrument lighting, and it rolled on special Turbo-Allot wheels.

Two powertrain choices were available: a (required in California) Oldsmobile-built 185-bhp, 403-cid V-8 driving through a three-speed Turbo Hydra-Matic or one of the last few Pontiac 220-bhp, 400-cid V-8s coupled to a 4-speed manual. Just 1,817 were built with the 400 V-8 and 5,683 with the 403, for a total of 7,500. With a list price of $10,620, the 10th Anniversary T/As were the first Firebirds with stickers topping $10,000.

1970 PORSCHE 914

Branded a Porsche for its 1970 U.S. debut, the mid-engine 914 was actually a co-production with Volkswagen, which supplied its 1.7-liter air-cooled flat four and many other components. The targa-top two-seater was quite practical for a "middie," with a roomy cockpit and a useful trunk at each end but didn't have the performance or racer-like handling expected of a Porsche, and access to its engine was difficult. A stiff $3,500 initial price also turned off critics and potential buyers.

Rightly concerned about its reputation, Porsche quickly cooked up a 914/6 version with a beefed-up chassis and a 2.0-liter, 110-bhp flat six straight out of the rear-engine 911, plus extra equipment including five-spoke 911 alloy wheels. Despite a much higher $6,100 base price, the 914/6—which could sprint 0-60 mph in under nine seconds and top 120

mph—was accepted as a "true" Porsche. But with 911s priced only some $1,000 higher, it never caught on and was gone by late 1971 after just 3,351 were built. The four-cylinder 914 continued with yearly improvements through 1976, racking up total worldwide sales of 115,596.

The 914 was always badged "VW-Porsche" for Europe, and even as it launched there in 1969, Porsche tried stuffing in a 300-bhp 3.0-liter flat eight from its Type 908 racer. The resulting "914/8" could hit 155 mph and rocket 0–60 in around six seconds. But Porsche concluded there was no market for it and gave up after building just one prototype, which was later given to Dr. Ferry Porsche as a 60th birthday present.

Porsche also considered a 916 with modified bodywork and a 190-bhp version of the 911's latest 2.4-liter six but built only 20 examples. Here, too, the reason was a likely lack of sales, especially as its price was projected at $15,000-$16,000. Skinny standard tires compromised the agility of four-cylinder 914s, but weekend racers were quick to realize the car's handling potential thanks to competition parts available from Porsche and aftermarket companies.

1972-73 PORSCHE 911

The Porsche 911 got its air-cooled flat-six stroked to 2.4 liters for 1972, plus a one-year-only external flap for the engine-oil filler behind the right door. The familiar trio of T, E, and S models now claimed respective U.S. horsepower of 157, 185, and 210.

Porsche built 1,636 RS 2.7s, mainly for Europe, where the model was street legal. A few came to America, but its non-U.S.-emissions-compliant engine meant owners couldn't legally drive them on public roads. For 1973, U.S. 911s wore large front bumper guards (visible on the S Targa here) to meet that year's new five-mph front crash requirement. Posing with it is a 911E, which got new-design alloy wheels. At mid-year, base T models got standard fuel injection like other 911s, which improved drivability and bumped horsepower to 137 SAE net.

1973 PORSCHE
911 CARRERA RS

Built for Group 4 GT racing and reviving a historic Porsche name, the 1973 Carrera RS boasted a new 230-bhp 2.7-liter flat six, beefed-up chassis and lightweight coupe bodywork with broader fender flares, bold bodyside graphics, and a distinctive "ducktail" rear spoiler. Porsche built 1,636 RS 2.7s, mainly for Europe, where the model was street legal. A few came to America, but its non-U.S.-emissions-compliant engine meant owners couldn't legally drive them on public roads.

1974 PORSCHE 911

Typical of Porsche, the 1974-model 911s kept pace with U.S. regulations, gaining artfully designed "crash" bumpers and a cleaner new 2.7-liter version of the familiar air-cooled flat six. Models were shuffled to base, S, and a new American-spec Carrera with the show but not the go of the earlier European RS. Only the S and Carrera were offered for 1975-77, little-changed except for added standard equipment—and inflation-fuel prices that reached beyond $14,000. Even so, sales remained brisk.

1976 PORSCHE
911 TURBO COUPE

Storming onto U.S. roads for '76, Porsche's 911 Turbo coupe packed 234 bhp from a new turbocharged 3.0-liter flat six good for 4.9-sec. 0-6s, 13.5-sec. ¼ miles and 156 mph flat out. Bulging bodywork and a big "whale tail" rear spoiler made it easy to spot. For 1978, the Porsche Turbo's enlarged 253-bhp 3.3-liter engine improved drivability more than velocity. Still, this was the fastest roadgoing Porsche yet and thus a genuine "gotta-have" the world over.

1977 PORSCHE 924

Seeking a more viable entry level model, Porsche replaced the mid-engine 914 with the front-engine 924, which launched in America for 1977, two years after its European debut. Porsche had originally designed it to be a Volkswagen but took it back after VW declined it, though Porsche tapped VW-owned Audi to handle assembly. Riding a 94.5-inch wheelbase, the 924 broke more new ground for Germany's premier sports-car builder with a water-cooled, overhead-cam VW/Audi 2.0-liter four cylinder with 95 horsepower in initial U.S. tune. A thin propshaft connected it to a manual four-speed rear transaxle, a layout that helped balance fore/aft weight distribution. A modern all-independent suspension provided handling that most reviewers judged excellent. Also new for Porsche was a hatchback coupe body style, whose big, curved rear window lifted for easy cargo access.

Despite its mixed parentage, the 924 was more readily accepted as a Porsche than the 914 had

been, and it proved more popular. Still, critics carped about engine noise and tepid acceleration, especially with the optional automatic transmission. Porsche responded in 1978 with a manual five-speed option, then later a 143-bhp 924 Turbo that cut 0-60 mph by some four seconds to around 7.7. And Porsche itself built the Turbo, which suggested even better 924s were on the way—as indeed they were.

1978 PORSCHE 911 TURBO AND 911SC

In addition to a hot 3.3-liter 911 Turbo, the 1978 Porsche lineup included a freshened 911SC coupe and Targa with many features of the previous Carrera, including wider rear wheels, tires, and fenders. One new wrinkle was a normally aspirated 3.0-liter flat six with 172 SAE net horsepower, plus a broader torque spread that reduced the need to shift as much at low speeds. A stronger crankshaft improved durability, and adoption of catalytic converters helped satisfy U.S. emissions standards.

The one downside was record prices that approached $17,000 to start, reflecting at least a decade of inflation. The '79s cost even more—over $20,000 base—and much more with special options like the plaid upholstery on the Targa shown here. By now, some pundits were starting to think that regulations would soon catch up with the 911, but Porsche would keep defying conventional wisdom by keeping its evergreen rear-engine sports car fresh, fast, and desirable for decades to come.

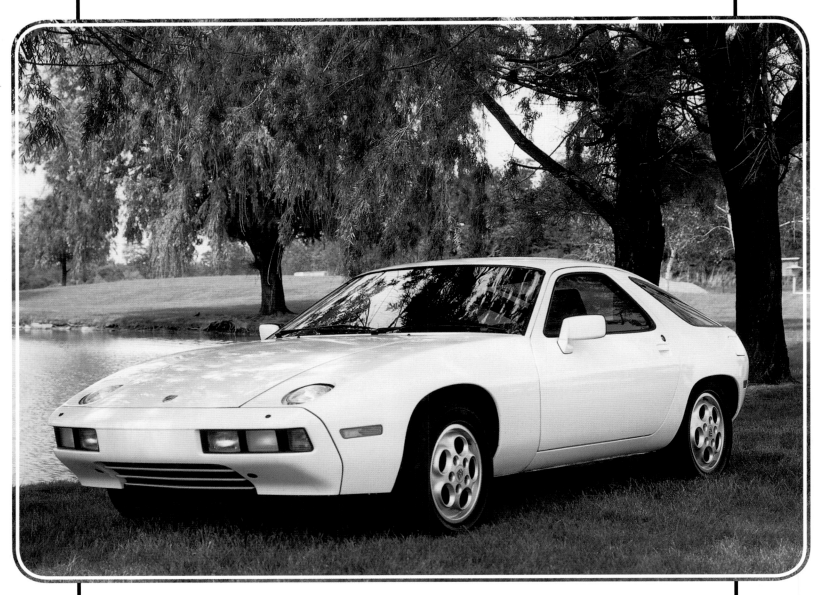

1978 PORSCHE 928

Though intended as a future rear-engine 911 re-placement, the Porsche 928 ended up a posh GT coupe. Its sleek 2+2 hatchback body seemed shrink-wrapped around a front-mounted, water-cooled V8—a first for a production Porsche—and a 924-like rear transaxle that helped fore/aft weight balance. Bowing in the U.S. for 1978, the 928 sent 219 horse-power through a five-speed manual or an optional three-speed automatic transmission.

Despite weighing a hefty 1.5 tons, it could shoot from zero to 60 mph in seven-plus seconds, run the quarter-mile in 15-16 seconds at 90 mph and hit 140 mph plus, and its four-wheel independent sus-pension and big disc brakes provided handling and stopping to match. Styling, by American Tony Lap-ine, featured slick body-color bumpers and Lambo-rghini Miura-style laid-back headlamps. Despite lofty pricing—initially $26,000—the 928 would survive into the mid-1990s. But it would never replace the evergreen 911.

1970 SAAB SONETT III

Unveiled at the 1970 New York Auto Show, the Saab Sonett III built on the previous Sonett II with a 1.7-liter German Ford V4, a new nose and tail by Italian Sergio Coggiola and an upgraded cockpit. The new styling improved aerodynamics but added weight that the larger engine couldn't offset, so its performance actually declined. Though offered mainly for the U.S., the Sonett III was dropped after 1974 due to slow sales and the planned North American phaseout of the parent Saab 96 sedan. Production ended at 8,351 units.

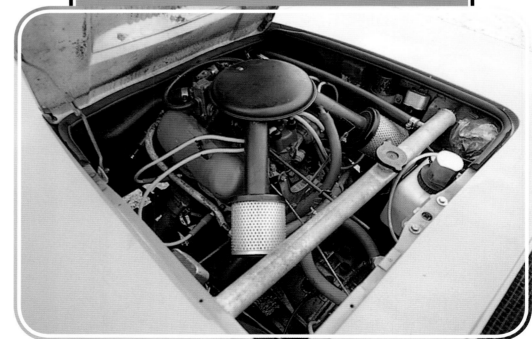

SAAB 96

Swedish Saabs—unlike rival Volvos—were decidedly weird in their early years, and that weirdness went well beyond their egg-shaped styling. Powered by a tiny two-stroke "corn-popper" 3-cylinder, they were also front-wheel drive before almost anything else save British Minis. The basic 96 model was upgraded for 1967 with a 1.5-liter four-stroke V-4 purchased from Ford, and that mild-mannered mill carried it through the 1970s. The V-4 generated 73 bhp in 1970 U.S. cars but for 1971 increased in size to 1.7 liters but with lower compression to meet U.S. emissions, and for '72 was rated at just 65 bhp SAE gross. The U.S. 96 was gone by 1973, but the larger 99 carried on until it was replaced by the all-new 900 in 1978.

1971 TOYOTA
CELICA ST HARDTOP COUPE

In 1971, Toyota introduced its Celica sport coupe, a car that many automotive magazines compared to the original Ford Mustang, which by 1971 had grown eight inches longer and 600 pounds heavier than the '65 original. Meanwhile, import coupes such as the Celica, Opel Manta, and Mercury Capri catered to buyers who wanted a sporty car that was smaller than early 1970s U.S. pony cars.

Toyota was building a reputation for dependable sedans, though it had built a few sports cars such as the tiny Sports 800 and the limited-production 2000GT, but the Celica was Toyota's first volume sport coupe. It was powered by a 113.4-cid (1.9-liter) four-cylinder engine that developed 108 bhp. A four-speed manual transmission was standard, as were front disc brakes. The notchback two-door hardtop

rode on a 95.5-inch wheelbase; and its curb weight was a reasonable 2,290 pounds. The base price was also reasonable at $2,598, and U.S. sales were brisk at more than 17,000 that first year.

In its first exposure to the Celica, *Motor Trend* was impressed with the styling, interior, standard equipment, and build quality. Its long hood and short rear deck were reminiscent of an American pony car, and its interior was well executed with reclining bucket seats, nylon carpet, and full instrumentation. MT found its performance acceptable at 12.7 seconds 0-60 mph but was less impressed with its handling due largely to its nose-heavy 59-percent-front/41-percent-rear weight distribution and narrow 165SR13 tires on small 13-inch wheels.

TOYOTA CORONA

Toyota's mid-range Corona, originally launched in 1957, played an important role in the brand's North American success after its 1964 U.S. debut with a 90-bhp 4-cylinder and numerous standard features. A redesigned Corona introduced in 1970 offered two-door hardtop coupé, four-door sedan, and station wagon body styles. The Corona was redesigned again in late 1971 and mildly restyled just one year

later, but (unlike most competitors) it would remain rear-wheel drive.

Greatly aided by the fuel crises of 1973 and 1979, the 1970s were Corona's high point in North America. August of that year brought a Gen V Corona in Japan, which came to America for '74 with a 2.2-liter 4-cylinder. North American models had longer bum-

pers (hiding recoverable bumper shocks) to meet five-mph impact standards and gained standard radial tires in 1975.

Introduced in Japan in late 1978, the 1979 fifth-generation Corona wore a boxier design and maintained its rear-drive layout. All models rolled on MacPherson strut front and four-link trailing arm rear suspension with a Panhard rod, except for the wagon, which used leaf springs, and disc brakes were standard equipment on all models. The last Corona marketed in the U.S., it was replaced for 1983 by the similar-size but front-wheel-drive Camry.

1973 TRIUMPH SPITFIRE

The Triumph Spitfire was a great low-cost way to go racing in its day. About all you had to do was optimize the engine, ditch the windshield, and bolt on a rollover bar and suitable rubber.

U.S. Spitfires from 1973 used the same 1500cc engine as contemporary MG Midgets, both sports cars having by then come under the British Leyland banner. Post-'73 Spitfires also got "1500" decals for nose and trunklid, two-inch wider axle tracks, a more coherent dashboard, and reclining bucket seats. Fittingly, the revised rear-end styling introduced with

the 1970 Mark IV update was done by Giovanni Michelotti, who'd shaped the original Spitfire. Unfortunately, BL took a cheap approach to meeting 1970s U.S. safety and emissions standards, so performance steadily declined, bottoming out in 1974 with just 57 horsepower and 0–60-mph times close to 16 seconds. Even so, U.S. sales remained healthy enough to keep the Spitfire alive into 1980, when production economics and rising red ink forced BL to give up on traditional sports cars altogether. Ironically, the Spitfire would be a model for the popular Mazda Miata of the 1990s.

1976 TRIUMPH TR7

Even while phasing out its Spitfire and TR6, Triumph launched a new sports car unlike any it had built before. Dubbed TR7, it came to the U.S. in 1976 as a unibody coupe with a 2.0-liter overhead-cam four good for 86-90 horsepower. The engine was from the parts bins of parent British Leyland, as were the standard front-disc/rear-drum brakes, all-coil suspension with front struts and a live axle on radius arms and the manual four-speed and optional five-speed overdrive transmissions. A three-speed automatic was also available as an American-market must. Despite riding a three-inch-shorter wheelbase, the TR7 was about as long as the TR6 and somewhat wider, so its cockpit and cargo space were uncommonly good for a two-seater.

But most agreed that its styling was not so good. Originating with an off-hand sketch by BL designer Harris Mann, it sought to emulate the "flying wedge" look of contemporary Italian exotics. But it didn't connect with most buyers, notwithstanding ad claims to the contrary. A convertible arrived in 1979 looking somewhat nicer, but consistently sub-par workmanship and BL's increasingly publicized troubles hampered TR7 sales, especially in the vital U.S. market, and the addition of V-8-powered TR8 models didn't help. As a result, Triumph was forced to abandon sports cars in late 1981.

In 1974, Volkswagen made a historic turn from air-cooled, rear-mounted engines to water-cooled front engines and front-wheel drive for its all-new compact Golf, which arrived in America in 1975 as the VW Rabbit. Then the "hot hatch" segment was born in 1976 when Europeans got a GTI version of the Golf with a more powerful engine and sport suspension, and its combination of sporty moves and family- car practicality proved popular. Americans wouldn't get a Rabbit GTI until 1983, and '84 was the last year for that first-generation GTI.

1976 VOLKSWAGEN
GOLF GTI

VOLVO 140, 160, 240, AND 260 SERIES

In 1967, Sweden's Volvo began designating its cars with three digits. The first digit was the series, the second its number of cylinders, the third its number of doors. So, the 1970 144 four-door and 145 wagon were powered by a 4-cylinder engine (which was enlarged to 2.0 liters for 1969) and the 164 sedan by a 3.0-liter six. They got an available 122-bhp fuel-injected version of the 4-cylinder and styling tweaks (including the long-running diagonal chrome bar across the grille) for 1971 and more for '72 before a major facelift for 1973. Then came safety upgrades, larger (U.S-legal) bumpers and a U.S.-emissions-compliant 109 bhp version of the four for '74.

The 140 and 160 series evolved into the "shovel-nosed" 240 and 260 series for 1975 with MacPherson-strut front suspension and power rack-and-pinion steering among the many safety and engineering improvements. For 1976, the 265 DL became the first six-cylinder-powered Volvo wagon, then the sporty 242 GT and a new OHC 4-cylinder arrived for '77. The 1979 model year brought a full facelift front and rear and a six-cylinder diesel engine.

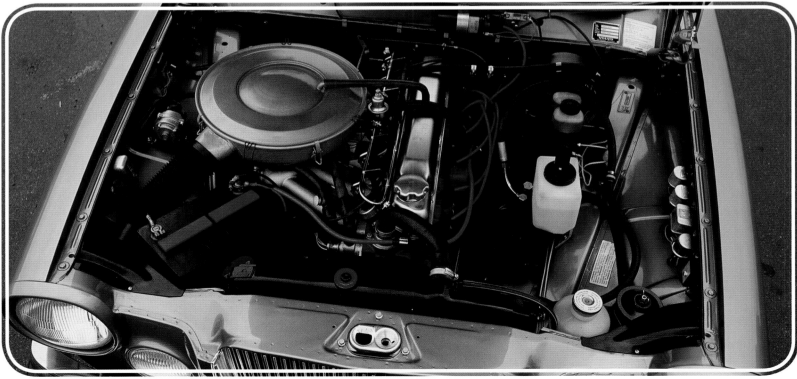